TOW TRUCK KINGS

Secrets of the Towing & Recovery Business

ALLAN T. DUFFIN

published by

duffin|creative

los angeles

Published in the USA by
Duffin Creative
11684 Ventura Blvd #205
Studio City, CA 91604
Visit us on the Web at duffincreative.com

Cover photograph courtesy of Jared Fox, Bob's Garage & Towing, Painesville, Ohio (bobsgarageandtowing.com). Used with permission.

ISBN-10: 0692327177
ISBN-13: 978-0692327173

Printed in the United States of America

Table of Contents

WHAT ARE YOU TOWING?

THE BUSINESS

INTERNATIONAL ISSUES

Introduction

As a freelance writer, I've covered a lot of different subjects. This collection of stories was selected from my work as a regular contributor to *Towing & Recovery Footnotes,* the newspaper of the towing industry, which publishes print and digital editions.

Tow Truck Kings features stories, tips, tricks, and information that makes for great reading for people already in the business, or as a primer or textbook for anyone interested in the industry. I've included chapters about accidents, different vehicles that are towed, attacks on towers, business practices, sales, storage, fuel prices, designing business websites, traffic incident management, legislation, import/export, recovery techniques used around the world, plus humorous stories from the road.

I hope you enjoy the book. If you have any questions, please feel free to contact me through my website at www.aduffin.com.

—*Allan T. Duffin*

Sold!
Buying a Tow Truck?
Here's What the Salespeople Have to Say

Whether you've spent decades in the towing business or are about to open your first shop, purchasing equipment for your company can be a nerve-wracking and expensive process. How can you ensure that you buy the truck you need at the best possible price? To answer this question, we went straight to the source and asked distributors and salespeople for their advice. After all, establishing solid, lasting relationships with good retailers will ensure that you're always able to dispatch the right type of tow truck—wherever and whenever it's needed.

Tow truck distributors across the country work with a wide variety of customers, from single-vehicle businesses to giant corporate fleets. "I deal with shops that range from one person to 50- or 60-man operations," says Mike Alvino of DG Towing Equipment and Service. The New York-based company spent more than three decades in towing and automotive repair before becoming a distributor for Dynamic wheel-lift trucks. Alvino's phones ring constantly. "We get a lot of new guys, just starting in the business, who call me up to buy self-loaders. It's an easy

1

unit to operate and safe for the driver because they don't have to get out of the truck. The repo industry is big on our Dynamic self-loaders."

Several states to the south, Chris Taylor of Eastern Wrecker Sales in Clayton, N.C., sells rollbacks and wreckers manufactured by Jerr-Dan, a division of the Oshkosh Truck Corporation. "We're the oldest active distributor of Jerr-Dan equipment," Taylor notes. Eastern Wrecker was founded in 1969 and originally sold Holmes wreckers. Taylor's largest clients are corporations with huge fleets of transport equipment and multiple offices across the United States. "But," he says, "the small business owner remains our most consistent and important customer." Taylor highlights one example of Eastern Wrecker's successful sales approach: the company has sold equipment to succeeding generations of owners at the same tow companies, thereby cementing family-type relationships between seller and buyer.

Although distributors use many common marketing approaches to find and build a customer base, the focus can vary by sales region. "We use various publications for our print ads as well as direct mail and cold calling," notes Eben Brady, a sales manager at Santex Equipment Sales in San Antonio. Most of Brady's sales are in rollbacks, but he's also seeing an increase in sales of self-loading wheel lifts, which prove useful in quickly clearing freeway incidents. Brady also points to the effectiveness of Internet advertising. "One new market that has increased significantly is our Web site traffic," he says. To maintain solid contacts in the industry, Santex participates in local and state towing associations and product expos. "We really enjoy seeing our customers and their families at tow shows and other events."

Maintaining an aggressive outreach strategy is critical for newer distributors like Santex, whose customers operate primarily in central and southern Texas. "We try to concentrate on our local area first and foremost," says Brady. Santex is gradually stepping up its marketing as the company grows. Key to the plan is the construction of a brand-new sales facility, with a nationwide sales campaign to follow.

With so many different ways to reach potential customers—print media, television and Internet, among others—Brady also likes to spread the word the old-fashioned way. "My favorite type of advertisement is word-of-mouth," he says. "It's free, and if a customer is outthere recommending youto his friends,that really lets you know you are doingyour job."

In the city of Dallas, general manager Jean Steward of Tex-Star Equipment Sales spends a lot of time on the road. "I travel as often as possible to meet new people and show them our product," she says. This personal approach has paid off extremely well for the company: 65 percent of Tex-Star's business comes from repeat customers. Referrals account for approximately 23 percent of sales, while the remaining 12 percent of customers are brand new to the company.

Tex-Star distributes equipment built by Miller Industries, which includes the Century, Challenger, Champion, Eagle Claw and Holmes product lines. "We mount these on the chassis of the customer's choice except when building demos," says Steward. "In those instances I try to use all brands: Chevrolet, Ford, Freightliner, International and others." Steward sells equipment to private companies as well as the United States Army. On occasion, she says, Tex-Star also builds trucks for export overseas. Clients from the private sector range in size from one-truck operations to corporate fleets of 20 vehicles or more. "Most of our larger customers have trucks ranging from auto-loaders (repo units) to 60- to 75-ton rotators," she notes.

For Steward, follow-through after a sale is extremely important. "I try to let all my purchasers know that I support them and their business," she says. To keep current on their customers' needs, the staff at Tex-Star sponsors and attends multiple training schools. The company also supports the Texas Towing and Storage Association's educational courses, traffic incident management training and legislative efforts.

With such extensive knowledge and marketing firepower, the salesperson is well equipped to make a sale. But the road from initial pitch to final handshake can be a bumpy one. What can the potential customer do to make sure he or she purchases the right tow truck at a fair price?

First, salespeople recommend that customers gather as much information as they can about the type of truck they need: What will the truck be used for? What types of terrain and climate will the truck operate in? How much can you afford to spend? If you're starting a new company, do you have a sound business plan?

From a purely managerial standpoint, Chris Taylor of Eastern Wrecker Sales recommends that towing company owners ensure that they deal with legal issues immediately. "For example, having a truck with enough GVWR—Gross Vehicle Weight Rating, a federally mandated system of rating the capacity of a truck chassis—to carry your load both safely *and* legally is more important than ever. Getting one's company set up correctly—incorporating, for example—and getting the proper insurance and licensing will protect your investment."

Owners of startup tow companies need to be realistic in evaluating their market and budget. "If you are new to the business, you might not want to purchase a new $65,000 rollback—consider a more affordable used unit instead," says Taylor. "A used rollback at $30,000 might not have the warranty you get on a new one, but for that $35,000 savings you can afford to make some repairs. The lower investment can make the difference between turning a profit and just turning your wheels."

Steven Cline of Mountain State Truck Center in Denver finds that customers usually know what they want because they like the equipment they already have and want to buy something similar. Cline sells Ford F450, F550 and F650/750 trucks coupled with AATAC rollbacks, wreckers and self-loaders. Due to the weather and terrain in Colorado, nearly all of the F450/550 series trucks are of the four-wheel drive variety. Cline's largest clients boast fleet inventories of at least 65 vehicles. To ensure his customers target the truck they want at a price they can afford, Cline utilizes a software application from Ford Trucks that produces a detailed performance report. The report is generated from the customer's preferences for the truck body, the proposed model, and payload and performance requirements.

Western Wrecker Sales of Portland, Ore., offers trucks from the Miller Equipment line. During its 40-year history, Western Wrecker has grown to service all types of wreckers and carriers and maintains an extensive inventory of more than 47 new carriers and wrecker units. Owner Mike Reese provides some helpful advice: "When getting quotes from vendors, compare apples for apples by checking off each item: chassis, gross vehicle weight, make, model, special equipment and ratings on equipment. Last but not least, ask your friends for their experience with a particular vendor's service, warranty, work done promptly without an argument, and whether the vendor has a good supply of consumable parts. Good relationships are made by being honest about any deficiencies on trade-ins."

Those good relationships are critical not only to the success of a towing company but also to the longevity of the distributor. Poor sales mean a short life in business, so the sales force makes every effort to ensure that customers are treated properly. After all, "we *want* to sell you a piece of equipment," says Chris Taylor. "Even more, the best equipment dealers want to establish a good working relationship with you. Why? For one thing, it helps us to sell you more equipment.More than that, it helps us to sell you the *right* equipment."

Taylor places a premium on detailed and constant communication: "Talk to us. Help us understand your goals, what you need to tow or to haul, what kind of budget you have, how soon or often you need to buy, and what kind of financing you need. That way we can offer you a range of options that you might not have thought about. And don't be embarrassed if you are just starting out or have a smaller budget. All of our customers are important to us." In addition, Taylor encourages customers to examine the distributor's service capabilities. "Ask to see our parts and service department. Ask about our installation department. Go to our website and download the brochures available there. And come look at our equipment."

Haggling over price can cause monumental headaches for both the salesperson and the customer. Santex's Eben Brady recommends a common-sense approach: don't buy a piece of equipment just because it was the least expensive product available. "Look over the unit's specifications to make sure it will do the job you want it to do," he says. Mike Alvino of DG Towing Equipment agrees. "Know exactly where you want to be. Do you want to do repo, regular towing, or something else? Keep to your needs. Don't overbuy."

Brady notes that most of his customers have done their homework and understand the truck specs they need. Since it's his job as a salesperson to ask as many questions as possible, Brady often helps fine-tune customer requirements. For example, he sometimes helps clarify differences among trucks with lighter GVWs. "Some customers get fooled by the lighter GVW trucks," he says. "I try to help by explaining the difference between a 19,500 GVW truck and its capacities versus a 26,000 GVW—and why the 26,000 GVW is going to cost more."

Technology changes as the years roll by, so Chris Taylor stresses the importance of keeping up with the times. Customers need to stay advised of changes in equipment. According to Taylor, Oshkosh Truck Corporation, the parent company of Jerr-Dan, has spearheaded improvements in rollback and wrecker design which have lowered operating costs and boosted safety. As an example, Taylor points to Jerr-Dan's maintenance-free, no-lube slide pad system as a cost- and time-saving device that was introduced in recent years.

On an emotional level, Eben Brady advises customers to "make sure that you feel goodabout the distributor you purchase the unit from. Make sure they are goingto take care of you after the purchase is made." Jean Steward agrees: "Towers need to always feel assured that they are getting the best price on the front end (purchase) and on the back end (trade). Always ask about the selling price prior to letting on that you have a trade. This keeps everyone honest. The tower needs to know he is getting the best price—and that the sales price is not being artificially inflated into more profit for the seller just so he can make it look like he is giving more for the trade than he really is."

A constant theme echoed by salespeople is a genuine concern for the customer and his or her business. "I want only what is best for the customer," says Steward. She offers a simple, practical piece of advice: "Even if you do not purchase equipment from us, make sure you purchase equipment that will be right for your company and its needs."

As always, for the salesperson, building trust with the customer is the key to success. "Selling is built on relationships," says Eben Brady. "I believe that staying in touch with your customers as much as possible is essential to keeping a strong client base." Chris Taylor feels that customers should feel comfortable enough to lean on their sales representatives when needed: "Take your time, take advantage of the knowledge of old hands like ourselves, and evaluate your market and your budget carefully."

In the end, the tow truck distributor or salesperson has the same goal as the customer does: get the right equipment into the right hands. "I live by being honest and forthright in this business," says Jean Steward. "If I do not or cannot provide the best equipment for the purchaser I will

6

refer them to someone who can.Ultimately, I like to be able to sleep at night and get up and look in the mirror with no regrets in the morning."

Ralph Weber:
Strategic Business Management
for Towers

Towing company owners wrestle with a myriad of paperwork—bills, receipts, insurance statements, legal issues, taxes, to name a few. Between shuffling paper and dispatching trucks, maintaining an effective business plan is critical to ensuring a healthy future for the company. How can a towing firm save money on its taxes? What types of health insurance plans can employees choose from? What other ways can a towing business manage its finances more effectively?

Ralph Weber wanted to provide clear, concise answers to these questions. So he hosted a seminar, "Strategic Business Management and Planning for Towers," in Chattanooga, Tenn. For $295—a portion of which Weber donated to The International Towing and Recovery Hall of Fame and Museum, which co-sponsored the event—towers from across the nation spent a day learning about the "business of the business."

The seminar taught towers how to manage risk, reduce expenses and taxes, and "let your business be your retirement plan," says Weber. "In order to maximize your profit and the value of your business, you need to understand cash flow and the tax code," he adds.

The full-day event kicked off at 7:30 A.M. with coffee and pastries. Two 45-minute sessions followed. The first session focused on the different types of business entities, including corporations, LLCs, partnerships and sole proprietorships. The second session dealt with calculating variable and fixed costs.

After a short break, Weber hosted additional sessions about financial statements, business plan development, saving money and reducing taxes, protecting assets from creditors, retirement planning, and more. Due to the success of the Chattanooga seminar, Weber plans to continue them on a regular basis.

The Road to Route Three

What encouraged Weber to sponsor seminars like this one? In 1995 he opened Route Three Life Health Disability, Inc., a Paso Robles, Calif.-based firm that provides insurance and financial services to the towing industry. Today Route Three has five staff employees and 25 brokers—seven in Canada and 18 in the United States. All have interesting backgrounds—for example, Peter Crittenden, who operates in North Carolina, is a 25-year Army veteran and former Green Beret.

Thanks to modern technology, companies like Route Three are able to cover a lot of ground and base their staff members in different locations. Tess St. Clair, the vice president of administration, handles issues regarding claims from the home office, while billing and administrative functions are located in Niagara Falls, Canada. The company accountant works out of San Francisco.

Focusing on towers

Why did Weber choose to work with the towing industry instead of another field of business? "I was a recovery technician in the Army for eight years," he explains. After he left active duty, Weber spent five years at the American Automobile Association supervising emergency road service. So, naturally, "When I started my insurance agency, I decided to specialize in the towing industry," he says. (Weber's new seminar was inspired by a course that he taught at AAA.)

Recognizing that proper training is as important to financial consultants as towers, Weber obtained his Registered Employee Benefit Consultant (REBC) designation in 1999. That certification, awarded through The American College in Bryn Mawr, Penn., gave Weber the background to work with pensions and retirement plan funding, installation and administration; group medical plans; long-term care; executive compensation and personnel management.

Armed with an REBC, Weber continued his professional education. Five years later he received his Certified Financial Planner (CFP) license. "I'm one of only 1,250 people in the U.S. and 76 in Canada with similar credentials," he says, adding that REBC is the highest designation available in the employee benefits field.

Towers might be surprised to learn that Weber's other training includes not only an accounting degree but seven years of management training with the McDonald's Corporation. Weber is a graduate of Hamburger University, the McDonald's Corporation's facility for operations training and leadership development in Oak Brook, Ill.

Health insurance

Since launching Route Three, Weber has worked with a variety of towers, offering group benefits and planning services. Weber's clients include Gary and Donna Coe, co-owners (with Donna's son, Jim Walsh) of Fleet Sales West, Sherwood, Ore., Golden West Towing Equipment in Anaheim, Calif.; Competition Wheel Lift in Los Angeles; and Chevron West in Sacramento. Weber notes that Route Three is the largest provider of health insurance for towers in North America.

A few years ago the Coes came to Weber for help in providing health care to their employees. The Coes needed to keep careful track of the laws in both of the states where they have tow truck distributorships. "It can be daunting to stay on top of the regulations," notes Donna Coe. In addition, "There is a significant need for clear explanation and patience with the process of ensuring that our employees have a grasp of their coverage and its limitations," she says.

After some discussion, the Coes engaged Weber and Route Three to coordinate health care plans for their dealership employees. "In order to provide health care benefits to our employees, it is critical that the plans be affordable and that we have strong support from our agency," says Coe.

More in the bank account

One of Weber's main goals is to save towers money. "If you own a company, you need to know how to get more money out of it," he says. Weber states that by assisting tow companies with business planning and helping them with their taxes, he saves the average towing company between $1,500 and $2,500 per employee each year. "So a 10-employee company should save about $20,000 a year," he explains.

Perhaps $20,000 sounds to good to be true. "I talk to towers every day," says Weber," and sometimes—I kid you not—when I show them how they can save $20,000, they tell me no thanks. Because they do not want to lose the tax deduction." However, this isn't the case, says Weber: "Towers make good money, and thosespend the time learning how to plan properly realize this profit," says Weber. "Those who don›t learn will continue to struggle financially."

During his many years supporting the towing industry, Weber has seen a number of business mistakes: "Not understanding the difference between cash flow and deductible expenses, and not understanding cost per call," he says. "Due to this, they sometimesmake rash decisions in purchasing and often overpay for some services." In addition, Weber cautions tow company management to avoid delegating financial responsibilities to employees who do not have the same vested interest as the owner.

Saving on accountant's expenses can also keep the books in the black. "An ounce of planning is worth a pound of accounting," says Weber. "Remember, the average CPA has 2,000 clients. If they work eight hours a day, 50 weeks a year, they have only one hour per client." It is not a CPA's job to help business owners plan for their businesses, cautions Weber.

Weber's seminar program was a natural outgrowth of his concerns about these types of errors in judgment. By providing a comprehensive one-day course in business practices, he hopes to help towers avoid the pitfalls of many of their peers.

What does Weber think about the future of the towing industry? "It will be very bright for towers who keep pace with technology," he says. "Towers are by nature innovative and entrepreneurial, and the leaders will always do well. Those who understand the benefit of investing in their businesses will grow and prosper."

Truckers and Towers

How do truck drivers view the towing industry? On the average, quite favorably. "Today, many towers are better equipped to handle large tractor recovery," says Terry Fortner, associate vice president of claims for Nationwide Insurance. "This has allowed many recoveries without further damage to the truck or cargo." Truckers, insurance companies, and towers themselves all have thoughts on how to sustain and improve tow service to the trucking industry.

Scott Burrows, owner of Burrows Wrecker Service in Pendleton, Ky., warns towers that keeping a good reputation can be an uphill struggle. Burrows says that tow operators should treat truckers with the same regard as all other customers. "Sadly, most customers remember only their most recent tow," he says. "You can do 10 good jobs for someone, and then make one mistake—chip one fender or bend one piece of trim— and you're the most inept person they've ever met. How those types of situations are handled is what defines a good relationship between towers and their customers."

The truckers weigh in

Because breakdowns requiring a tow happen only periodically, truck drivers remember their experiences with towers quite vividly. Trucker Mark Trail recalls a tow truck driver who got him back on the road at night on a dangerous highway. Trail was delivering equipment to the Peterbilt Motors Company when his rig gave up the ghost. "I had a tow truck driver help me down in Texas just outside of Dallas," he says. "I blew my motor right on the side of the highway."

The loop around Dallas/Forth Worth was crowded with speeding traffic, so the tower got right to work. "He risked his neck to get my truck out of there, trailer and all," says Trail. "When we did get to the Peterbilt dealership in Fort Worth, he backed it up along a fence like a pro."

Trail says that despite the inconvenience of having a disabled truck, watching a tow truck operator in action was an enlightening experience. "I gained a lot of respect for those guys because of the skill that driver showed."

A veteran trucker and dispatcher with over three million miles of road behind him, W.J. "Andy" Andrews writes about his experiences on his blog, "Flat Tire" (19wheeler.blogspot.com). "For the most part," he says, "any experiences I've had with tow truck operators have been positive." Andrews recalls only two instances when towing service was less than satisfactory: when a careless tow operator damaged a truck bumper, and when another stopped to eat breakfast while his client waited for him to arrive on scene.

Andrews has worked with a variety of towers over the years and has watched various types of equipment in use. "I've worked with operators who had radio-controlled booms and some who had old swing booms," he recalls. His most memorable tow involved an operator in North Carolina who used a World War II surplus tow truck.

Andrews previously worked for a company that delivered new trucks to dealers and fleets around the country. "In many instances the undecking was done with tow trucks," he says. "Some towers we dealt with were regulars that were very expert; others we had to guide through the process."

These days Andrews works a different job in the trucking industry. "As a night dispatcher," he says, "I've had to find a tow truck for a breakdown. I use a Service Locator and the Truckdown vendor locator (www.truckdown.com) as sources for information. In some cases when weather is bad, the wait can be long." Andrews adds that truckers need to understand that towers are at their busiest during poor weather conditions, and adjust accordingly.

Thomas Wiles, known as "Trucker Tom," creates video and audio podcasts from the cab of his truck as he travels around the United States. Wiles notes that his experiences with tow truck drivers have been positive. The towing companies that Wiles has dealt with "tend to be small mom and pop operations," he says, "and their drivers tend to be friendly and efficient. When I'm home for time off, I pay to drop and park my trailer at a local towing company since I can't park it at home."

By contrast, Daniel Kupke, a truck owner/operator from Illinois, has faced difficulties in getting a tow. Kupke is currently working for a contractor in Iraq and needed his Peterbilt truck towed to Atlanta for some mechanical work after the holiday season. Unfortunately the tower he contacted never called him back, and Kupke might need to drive the rig himself once he returns from overseas. He's surprised that a tower would turn down such lucrative business. "This would have been a big chunk of money for them," says Kupke.

Tower Burrows is saddened when he hears stories like Kupke's. "Our relationship with the trucking industry should be almost hand-and-glove," says Burrows, "because we're probably better identified as a trucking company with a specialized fleet." The things that concern trucking companies, says Burrows — highways, regulations fuel prices, equipment costs — are shared by towing companies as well.

Burrows points to the "price per pound" billing method as an example of how towers can confuse truckers. "Almost no trucking company understands 'price per pound,' and towers do a very poor job in explaining it," says Burrows. "Although I do not use or recommend the PPP method, it works well for some recovery operators. It works even better if the customer is given a theoretical understanding of the rationale behind the formulas, and how those charges are fairly administered."

When a trucker is given an invoice for, say, 11.5 cents per pound and isn't schooled in how to read such a bill, "it does little to instill confidence in the recovery operator's customer service skills," says Burrows.

Insurance claims on big rigs

The insurance companies have a different but just as helpful perspective on the relationship between truckers and towers. At Nationwide Insurance, basic transport claims are handled with little fanfare. "If the tow is requested, as the type requested to move a heavy truck to a body shop from a storage yard, our relationships and ability to receive accurate costs and detail is excellent," says Terry Fortner, associate vice president of claims.

On the other hand, when an insurance claim deals with recovery and cleanup of an accident scene, Fortner notes that at times, unfortunately, the relationship between Nationwide and certain towing services can become adversarial. For example, explains Fortner, towers' billing documentation is sometimes lacking in detail, causing difficulty for the insurance company as it attempts to verify charges. "As a result," laments Fortner, "we have found the need to use an auditing service to determine the viability of pricing."

Recent focus on ecological awareness has led to towers billing for environmental cleanup services. Again, the insurance companies ask for clearer documentation: "While we understand the need for environmental clean up as a result of fuel spills or type of cargo," says Fortner, "many times the towers cannot provide proper environmental cleanup documentation."

At the Ohio Insurance Institute, a trade association representing over 35 property and casualty insurance companies that operate in the state, staff members try to help people better understand insurance and related safety issues. According to Dean Fadel, vice president for government affairs, OII has dealt with solid, honest towers as well as unscrupulous ones. "We have received numerous examples from our members of charges for simple transport truck tows, some of which are over $20,000 and covered a short distance," says Fadel. "Other dishonest towers have included extra charges if it's raining or snowing or if a door on the vehicle being towed needs to be open or shut." Some companies have received invoices from towers in amounts that are over double what the vehicle may be worth.

Because OII assists truckers with problems, the organization receives more complaints than kudos, but Fadel is quick to praise the towers who do their jobs the right way. "Obviously there are good players and bad players in every game," he explains. "In Ohio the good, honest towers are being lumped in with the bad ones. The honest operators need to speak out for proactive measures to bring professional standards to the industry and ultimately weed out the bad actors."

So how can towers help insurance companies process claims more efficiently? Fortner recommends that towers "provide details as to what was necessary, conditions, position of the vehicle, and difficulties in recovery and tow of the disabled vehicle." For large or complex recovery operations, Fortner adds that photographs of the recovery operation and the procedures involved would be a great benefit to the insurance companies. Most problems with insurance claims center around a lack of detail in billing, explaining why the amount of labor and equipment was needed to recover a disabled truck.

In addition, says Fortner, towers need to remember that if a claims specialist asks for more information, it doesn't necessarily mean that the insurance company is questioning the validity of the bill. To the contrary, "it may mean that we simply do not have enough information to make an evaluation," he explains.

"We want to provide the best service to our customers," says Fortner, "and pay the fair and appropriate payment for services rendered." Providing detailed and accurate billing and information will go a long way toward helping insurance companies handle claims for recoveries involving big rigs. Fadel offers additional advice: "Be honest and reasonable." Adds Fortner: "It's really helpful if towers see us as a necessary partner to keep our shared customers on the road, instead of an adversary looking to reduce their invoices unfairly."

Making improvements

Truckers also have some helpful hints for the tow operators they see on the road. Trucker Jimmy Frost, a company driver for 16 years, notes that good communication with the customer is a must. "Sometimes the tower would say he'd be out there in an hour or two," recalls Frost, "but then three or four hours go by, we're sitting on the side of the road and don't have a clue about when the tow truck would get to us." Frost recommends that tow truck drivers keep in touch if their schedules change: "If you say you're going to be there in an hour, be there in an hour," he says. "Please keep us in the loop."

Frost says that safety departments of trucking companies are sometimes faced with towing rate structures that are highly suspect. "They know the equipment is expensive and the liability coverage is expensive," explains Frost, "but sometimes the towers are profiteering." In one instance, Frost remembers an overturned big rig in Ohio costing around $27,000 to recover. But in general, Frost notes that many tow truck drivers are former truckers, and that there is a healthy respect between the two groups.

Trucker Mark Trail recommends that towers keep their CB radios turned on. "There are plenty of times when a truck driver is in a jam," he says. "It would be a big help if we could reach out to tow trucks by CB."

Debbie Martin, director of operations for Driver Bridge LLC, a recruiting service in Nashville, Tenn., searches out and screens applicants for large trucking companies. "At Driver Bridge we have noticed that drivers of tow trucks eventually want to move into other areas of the transportation industry," says Martin. "However, tow truck drivers seldom realize that they must have tractor trailer experience along with the tow truck driving to qualify by many company standards. A driver must have 'combination' experience."

Without a blended resume, Martin says, the only true qualification a tower will have is a Class B license. Martin also notes that many trucking companies have stringent requirements due to Department of Transportation requirements as well as insurance company audits. To keep a driver marketable within the industry, Martin recommends that drivers work part-time for a temp agency to keep their tractor-trailer experience fresh, make use of combination vehicles if your company has them, and to keep criminal and driving records (including those for personal vehicles) as clean as possible. Professionalism, appropriate dress, grooming, good manners, and use of signals go a long way, adds Martin.

Burrows says that the towing industry should be able to speak with one voice, similar to the trucking industry, which has umbrella organizations like the American Trucking Association, Owner-Operator Independent Drivers Association and, in his home state, the Kentucky Motor Transport Association.

"Tow companies should also consider joining their state's motor carrier association," adds Burrows. "How better to network with new customers and service existing fleets?" Better yet, says Burrows, towers can not only get certified and trained by the Towing & Recovery Association of America and WreckMaster, but also join a motor club like the California State Auto Association, which teaches customer service techniques.

Going after unscrupulous towers will also improve the relationship between truckers and towers. "We as towers need to continue to force those who charge indiscriminately and unfairly to be accountable for their behavior," says Burrows.

The legal side agrees. "Just like tractor trailer drivers, tow truck drivers are professionals," says Michael Jeffcoat, an attorney in Lexington, S.C., who represents professional drivers as part of his casework. "That's the bottom line. As professionals, tow truck drivers are usually held to a much higher standard than the average driver of a non-commercial vehicle."

"In the legal system," says Jeffcoat, "whoever has a hand in creating a potential danger is required to protect against that danger. Tow truck drivers need to not only be good drivers, but they need to be rested and in good physical and mental condition so that they can properly do their job."

Finally, maintaining strong friendships with truckers pays off in the end. Burrows recommends that towers consider a visit or a care package sometime during the year, and not just during the holidays.

"The praises are from those trucking companies who have had the good fortune to be served by a provider that gives them exceptional service," says Burrows. "They are quick to tell anyone soliciting their business that 'their' tower will remain their tower until one or the other goes out of business."

Fit to Be Towed:
Health and Fitness for Tow Truck Drivers

Disclaimer: The health-related information provided in this article is for educational and informational purposes only. For tips on how to improve your specific situation, please visit your health care provider.

You spend a lot of time on the road. How's your health? Driving a tow truck is a tough job with heavy demands that, left unchecked, can eat away at a tower's well-being and attitude. "If you're on call, you might be working at almost any hour, day or night," says Teresa Moore, M.D., a family physician in Charlotte Court House, Va. "With those kinds of demands on your system, your health is directly related to your work and lifestyle habits." Balancing a busy job with the other daily requirements of life — family responsibilities, fitness, nutrition, and managing stress, to name a few — is a lot for anyone to tackle. So how can towers effectively maintain or improve their health while on the job?

Perhaps no one sees a greater variety of health issues than managers who deal with on-the-job injuries. Colleen Deutsch, the worker's compensation manager for the nation's largest towing company, United Road Towing in Mokena, Ill., coordinates among 10 divisions across the United States. Each division in the network has its own claim handler who works directly with the main support office, where Deutsch monitors "every incident, every doctor's appointment, and any litigation that might arise — from the time the injury occurs until the time it closes with the insurance company."

Although after 17 years in the business she's seen just about everything, sometimes an injury still causes Deutsch to raise an eyebrow. "Last March, for the first time, I actually had a driver who slipped on a banana peel," she recalls. "He sprained his wrist." That incident had its humorous side, "but it's important to know that fifty percent of the injuries we deal with are slips and falls," she says. "Busy tow truck drivers have slipped on everything from ice to gravel to oil on the roadway." In addition, towers have twisted their ankles and received contusions from banging their elbows on obstructions. Other common injuries include back problems resulting from pushing, pulling, or bending their bodies in order to hook up a vehicle.

One of the key health concerns for towers — and a huge concern for medical experts as well — is the prevention and treatment of lower back problems, which are common among people who spend most of their workday in a sitting position. "Sitting, in general, is the least desirable position for the lower back," says Chuck Berg, D.C., a chiropractor based in River Vale, N.J., and author of the new book *Is Your Lifestyle Killing You?* "Towers spend a good part of their day in a relatively sedentary position. That's how we spend the bulk of our time while driving."

According to Berg, sitting — far more than standing or lying down — increases pressure on the lower discs of the spine. Deutsch notes that another reason for back problems among towers is the rapid rate of activity during recovery jobs. "At an accident scene, because there's a need to get vehicle traffic moving again, tow truck drivers are working at very high rates of speed," she says. "Sometimes in the rush to hurry and hook up a car, towers can twist their backs."

To improve and maintain their health, Berg first encourages towers to understand the effects of constant pressure exerted on the human body. "Most of us aren't really conscious about our day-to-day routine," he says. "I wake up, then sit down to have my breakfast. I get in my car, where I sit as I drive to work. I get to work, where I sit all day. I sit for lunch, drive home in a sitting position, sit for dinner, then sit to watch some television."

Berg notes that advances in technology have driven Americans to spend much of their time in a sedentary position. If not addressed early enough, he says, this type of lifestyle can lead to arthritis as well as hip and lower back problems. For tow truck drivers, "these health issues can make them unable to do their jobs," which directly affects their business and salary.

Visiting a medical expert can be beneficial to towers who are experiencing back pain that is affecting their work. "Lower back problems need to be addressed by a physician to rule out not only serious medical conditions such as disc herniations or osteoarthritis but also other possible causes such as abdominal hernias," says Geoffrey Lloyd, D.O., a doctor of osteopathic medicine in Burbank, Calif. "Eventually these conditions can be physically debilitating and sometimes life-threatening."

There are different modes of treatment, and towers should choose the approach with which they're most comfortable. While M.D.'s might prescribe analgesic medicine (painkillers) or anti-inflammatory remedies coupled with an exercise and nutrition plan, osteopathic doctors like Lloyd add the use of their hands to assist with the body's natural healing capabilities to reduce pain, ease muscle tension, and improve circulation.

In addition to visiting a medical professional, Berg notes that there are a number of things that towers can do immediately to put them on the road to better physical conditioning. Berg recommends that tow truck drivers invest in lumbar seat cushions to help alleviate stress on the spine. Simple and inexpensive, lumbar cushions "gently increase the curve in the lower back," says Berg, who notes that most chairs force the spine into an unnaturally straight position. The seat pillow helps the spine remain in its normal contour.

Although it would be helpful for towers to spend 30 to 40 minutes of their workday exercising, "this can be difficult if not impossible if you're on call and never know when you'll be needed at an incident site," says Moore. However, she and Berg offer one easy solution: "Get out of the truck as often as possible."

Just stepping out of the cab and moving around — a form of light exercise — can boost a tower's level of fitness. "Be consciously aware as you move your body," recommends Berg. In addition, he says, towers should make sure that they bend at the knees when performing activities such as hooking up a disabled vehicle. "Doing straight bends puts an enormous amount of tension on your lower back," he says.

Believe it or not, acting childish can actually help with stress management. Berg recommends that towers relieve shoulder tension by shrugging. "While you're driving, raise your shoulders to your ears, like a little kid saying, 'I don't know.'" Because the human head weighs 14 to 16 pounds, the neck and upper back muscles undergo significant amounts of stress. "Remember that you're carrying an average men's bowling ball on your neck," says Berg. Quick exercises like shrugging and deep breathing send a signal to the body that "life is not an emergency." Lloyd notes that a number of simple "on-the-job" exercises can be squeezed into the workday whenever there's time, including jumping jacks, sit-ups, and push-ups. "This takes a little more time and effort," he admits, "but it all depends on how motivated the driver is to stay healthy. That's the key."

What about external factors over which towers have little or no control? Climate, for example, plays a large part in a tower's overall health on the job. "Our drivers work in temperatures below zero all the way up to 115 degrees Fahrenheit," says Deutsch. She and Joe Braverman, general manager of E&R Towing in Markham, Ill., are careful to talk to their drivers on days with extreme temperatures. During hot days, says Deutsch, "we encourage our employees to wear light and loose-fitting clothing." E&R also provides ice water to each driver. When the weather is chilly, Deutsch reminds drivers to cover up, wear layers, and toss on a hat.

At G&S Service/I-80 Towing of Johnston, Iowa, owner Glenn Mikel stocks ANSI-approved clothing for the winter months and water and salt tablets for hot days. To avoid injuries, Mikel's staff regularly makes use of vehicle wash facilities to spray away oil and other contaminants that might cause someone to slip and fall. Leather gloves, hardhats, and an insistence on getting annual flu shots are also part of the company's efforts to make the job safer — and healthier — for every employee.

Safety extends to even the most basic maneuvers. "We teach our drivers how to get in and out of their trucks," says Mikel. "It sounds simple, but people forget sometimes. We remind our drivers not to jump out — to step out backwards instead of forwards so they don't accidentally slip and fall out of the cab." At E&R Towing, a monthly driver's roundtable reviews injuries as well as traffic incidents that occurred during the previous four weeks. "We discuss everything," says Deutsch. "If we have a driver who got out of his truck and didn't do a three-point hold, we talk about it. We stress safety every way we can."

This focus on safety as a way of improving health and morale also includes such tactics as placing signage at the exit to the tow yard. "We have a portable stop sign with a changeable message board," explains Braverman. On different days the board alerts drivers to weather conditions and important events: "It's raining today," "Don't forget your seatbelt," "School is starting." Newsletters and video presentations round out E&R's safety program.

One of the toughest parts of any workday — especially if it's spent primarily behind the wheel — is finding the time to eat. How can the busy tower make sure that he or she has food available when it's needed? "The best way to achieve this is to bring your own food in a cooler," says Lloyd. "Take 15 to 20 minutes the night before to prepare your food for the next day," adds Berg.

"Although it takes a greater effort on the part of the driver," says Lloyd, "the results will be life-long" because towers can make healthier food choices when preparing instead of purchasing their meals. If packing a lunch isn't feasible, Moore recommends visiting local convenience stores to purchase items like bottled water, yogurt, nuts, and whole or dried fruits. Managers of towing firms can help with this as well. At G&S Service, owner Glen Mikel orders food into the shop whenever possible. "We try to give our drivers time to get a good meal," explains Mikel.

What about using coffee as a pick-me-up? Despite its popularity, coffee can also cause problems in the workday. "Excessive coffee, with its caffeine, will increase the stress hormone known as cortisol," says Berg. "When cortisol increases in the body, so does insulin, which is a fat-storage hormone." So after having a lot of coffee, says Berg, "we are actually encouraging the body to gain weight."

He recommends sticking with water, which won't dehydrate the body like coffee does. Moreover, lack of water in the body can actually lead to problems with the lower back. "The average consumer doesn't drink much water at all," notes Berg, adding that the belief that "if I have 10 cups of coffee, that's equivalent to 10 cups of water" is common but incorrect. Soda — regular or diet — can also be a detriment to good health, as its phosphoric acid can lead to osteoporosis, in which bones in the human body lose calcium and other critical nutrients.

While dealing with the elements and sometimes-grouchy customers, towers are subjected to high levels of job-related stress. There are a number of simple things that towers can do to help alleviate the problem. "Deep breathing exercises before and after each call can help reduce stress immensely," says Lloyd. "Taking a few deep, measured breaths can lower blood pressure and increase oxygen to the brain.

Another benefit of this easy exercise is that it helps decrease the body's "fight-or-flight" response to stress. "By doing this," notes Lloyd, "you can reduce the excitatory portion of your body's autonomic nervous system. That's the part of your body that regulates unconscious activity like your heartbeat and your breathing." Moore agrees, adding that drivers who deal with cranky customers should remember that the anger is not really directed toward the tower and is instead the byproduct of an already stressful situation.

Crowded scheduling can be another culprit on the road to good health. "Time management is vital for drivers to be able to work efficiently and with appropriate breaks between jobs," says Lloyd. At G&S Service, owner Glen Mikel regularly encourages his drivers to get plenty of sleep and schedules at least one day a week off without any distractions from the company. Mikel has another, rather unique, solution: a Jack Russell Terrier named Jack. As friendly as he is furry, Jack helps lower stress in the shop by engaging the drivers to pet and play with him.

Small things like this on the part of management go a long way toward helping employees live a better life. "There is nothing more important than taking care of our employees," says Colleen Deutsch. "We're nothing without them." But in the end, personal health is up to the individual driver. Small things like simple exercises and carrying healthy snacks can make a huge difference in day-to-day life. As Berg notes, "It's all about the decisions we make to take care of ourselves."

Trauma Unresolved:
PTSD on the Road

A 16-year-old boy in Michigan is driving home. About a quarter-mile from his house he falls asleep at the wheel. His car rumbles over the centerline and collides with a loaded gravel hauler — 2000 pounds of car smashing into 139,000 pounds of truck. The gravel hauler crushes the car, metal scraping against metal, until the front bumper of the truck comes to a stop at the rear window of the car.

Paul Sheffer, owner of Paul's Collision & Towing, Inc., in Almont, Mich., got the call to haul away the mangled car. "We had to lift the truck off the car to get the car out," recalls Sheffer. "Then we had to rig lines to pull the front of the car off the boy to get him out of the car. I'm not sure were the boy's head was. I didn't look — but I know it wasn't attached."

Some towers never have to deal with recovery jobs like this one. And some towers have to live with the memory for the rest of their lives. The resulting trauma from experiencing this kind of tragedy, if not effectively dealt with, can develop into an ongoing condition known as Post Traumatic Stress Disorder, or PTSD.

Visions that never go away

The spectre of PTSD can haunt anyone exposed to a highly stressful or life-threatening situation. "Even if you only witness the aftermath of a horrific situation, you are at risk for developing negative symptoms associated with the traumatic scene," says Daniel Zimet, Ph.D., of Crossroads Psychological Associates in Columbia, Md. In addition to working with individuals and families, Zimet runs an adult group for persons coping with significant emotional and social hardships.

Though the term is often heard in a military context, PTSD isn't just experienced by combat veterans returning from war. "Early responders to violent and dangerous situations are particularly vulnerable to developing mental health problems related to what they have seen or had to do," says Zimet. "This is just as true for tow truck drivers as it was for responders to 9/11."

According to Zimet, the symptoms of PTSD include recurrent and intrusive thoughts about the event, anxiety and avoidance of anything reminding the person of the event, nightmares, mood changes such as feeling depressed, diminished interest in activities, feeling distant from people, and a disquieting feeling of being keyed-up or on edge.In more severe cases a person can forget large pieces of memory about the traumatic event and experience flashbacks, as well as feel a sense of being detached from his or her own body or mind.

These symptoms "are the responses of the body to help overcome danger," adds Dr. Elmer Maggard, a psychologist based in Booneville, Ky., who works at Navy Medical Center Portsmouth (Va.) with military personnel returning from combat. Maggard is also a former coal operator and trucking company owner. He classifies PTSD as having three primary types of symptoms.

First, PTSD sufferers re-experience the danger via flashbacks, intrusive memories, or dreams of the event. "The dreams are alarm responses," says Maggard. "Although they disrupt your sleep, they're the mind's way of waking you up to keep you aware of the danger until it's overcome. That means your spontaneous neurological reaction is to stay awake because the danger isn't over." The resulting sleeplessness can lead toincreased stresson the job.

In working with a military population, Maggard has found that "most PTSD is a result of wars that aren't over yet, or battles that we didn't win." How does a soldier or sailor overcome his or her PTSD, then? "You need to experience some sort of victory over the situation and overcome the danger," says Maggard.

If the situation remains unresolved, PTSD sufferers might begin to display the second general symptom of PTSD: an avoidance response to keep from being overwhelmed by the trauma. "It's a way for the mind and body to manage the amount of danger," says Maggard. "You might see soldiers laughing just before a battle, pranking on the battlefield, or see people reading or listening to music." All of these activities are ways to keep trauma — or impending trauma — from overwhelming the body and mind.

To guard against potential danger, the third symptom of PTSD is the increased arousal of the nervous system. "You have highly honed and tuned reactivity to any sign or indication that danger is present," says Maggard. "You'll get angry more quickly, run away faster, turn and fight faster. You'll be hyper-vigilant; you'll be scanning for danger."

Trauma on the road

Some towers have dealt with harrowing recovery jobs involving maimed or dead bodies. Jason Strickland, owner of Strickland Towing in Wellington, Kan., is one of them. "I have had several experiences with fatalities and seeing dead bodies, waiting on the coroner tocome out before we can do anything with the wreckage," he recalls. In two of those incidents, Strickland actually knew the victims. "I don't know that I suffered PTSD," he says, "but I did feel horrible for the families. Every time that we work a fatality my heart goes out to the families."

In Michigan, Paul Sheffer recalls another recovery job that has stuck with him through the years. Just before Christmas a mother was traveling home from a holiday party at work. She was drunk. Her car was stuffed with Christmas presents. "She hit a tractor trailer," says Sheffer, "and the truck nearly cut the car from the right headlamp to the left quarter panel."

When Sheffer arrived on scene, first responders were removing the body and "there was something on the road that I was not familiar with," he recalls. He asked Emergency Medical Services personnel what it was. "They confirmed it was brains," he says. He couldn't get the woman or her now-motherless children out of his head. "Those sad children weighed heavy on my heart," says Sheffer.

Though Strickland and Sheffer have accepted what they saw and have moved forward, some towers might be haunted for years by bloody accident scenes they've experienced. "The most important thing to understand about the so-called symptoms of PTSD is that they are the emergency response of the mind and body to danger," says Maggard. Under the right circumstances — in a combat zone, for example — PTSD symptoms work to help solve or overcome the danger that a person is facing. "You have to be aware of it, and you have to stay aware of it until the danger is gone," explains Maggard.

But in many cases, PTSD symptoms continue because the situation isn't resolved or is open-ended. Since they can't reverse the consequences of an accident, towers and first responders are highly susceptible to this problem. However, first responders have an advantage over the tow truck drivers: At an accident scene the first responders can have an impact on the extent of a victim's injury — and possibly save a life. So the danger that the first responders face can be mitigated or overcome simply by doing their job.

Towers, on the other hand, usually arrive at a bloody accident scene unable to resolve or affect the situation. "If the tragedy has already happened," says Maggard, "you're looking at an aftermath. The natural instinct is to prevent it or fix it. But once it's happened, you have neither opportunity as a tow truck driver." Thus the resulting psychological trauma — "the experience of being alone or outnumbered in the presence of danger or tragedy" — can continue to plague the tower.

The past catches up

Sometimes PTSD symptoms are the result not of road incidents but something else in a tower's past. Jonathan Ginsberg, an attorney in Atlanta, Ga., recalls a client who worked as a tow truck driver for about eight years. The man's PTSD "manifested itself in the form of flashbacks, overreaction to unexpected sounds like horns or street sounds, and problems interacting appropriately with customers and co-workers," says Ginsberg.

The tower spent every workday reacting to stimuli both physical and psychological. Noise was an issue. "Blaring horns and backfires would make him very jumpy and on edge," says Ginsberg. "These sounds would sometimes result in bad dreams and flashbacks." Honking horns and loud street noises — especially on hot days when he drove with the windows open — would result in nightmares when he went to sleep.

More important — and most crippling for a tower — were the man's problems interacting with customers. For example, when customers complained about delays in response time, arguments often ensued. In the shop, the tower had problems in relationships with his co-workers. In eight years on the job, he had minimal conversation with other drivers. The end result: his career in the towing industry ended sooner than it needed to.

Working through the Social Security system, Ginsberg was able to secure his client some disability support by providing evidence that the tower was suffering from PTSD that had begun on the battlefield many years before.

Solutions to the symptoms

If a tower suspects he or she is suffering from PTSD, it's important to deal with the issue as soon as possible. Don't keep the experience bottled up, say the experts. "These feelings should not be ignored as they can endure for a very long time — often years — and they can frequently get worse," notes Zimet. "Unfortunately," he adds, "many people choose to ignore or turn to negative choices like alcohol to cope with PTSD. This can affect your work, relationships with people, and overall health in a profound way."

"Your best choice is to communicate with someone about what you observed and experienced," says Zimet, "and learn techniques for managing your thoughts and stress."

Opening up about what you've seen can be difficult. Strickland, who's seen acquaintances die at accident scenes, notes that sometimes he stays quiet, mainly out of necessity in order to get the job done. "I think that I have become somewhatcallous toopening up my personal feelings and try to focus on the twisted metal part of the accident," he explains.

"Working a family member's or a friend's accident is much, much harder when myown personal feelings are involved," Strickland continues. "Whenwe work a fatality most of the time we don›t talk about it very much, and there are only a few of us who have actually seen a dead body on an accidentscene."

However, Strickland acknowledges that he and his staff do their best to share the pain that a difficult recovery job can trigger: "Most of the time if something is bothering us we all discussit at the end of the day," he explains.

At Tony's Wrecker Service, Inc., in Louisville, Ky., owner Nick Schade goes through the same thing with his employees. "We talk about what happened," he says, "but as far as any kind of outside professionals coming in, we haven't had the opportunity or need to do that so far."

Schade notes that his employees are often protected from viewing the gore of a horrible accident scene: "Usually we don't see too much of it — for example, the fire department has already cut the victim out of the wreck by the time we arrive," he explains. In addition, Schade does his best to cater to any employees who aren't comfortable responding to a bloody incident. Usually Schade will go himself instead of sending someone else.

At Five Seasons Auto Rebuilders, David Beer prepares his drivers accordingly. "All my drivers are told that any time they're in an uncomfortable situation, they're to call me immediately," says Beer. At that point, Beer can replace the driver at the scene, or — if the driver is all right with handling the situation — Beer follows up after the job. "We'll seek out the appropriate type of counseling for the driver," he says. "And they know that they can take days off."

Schade notes that a professional counselor would be useful in an area where there are a greater number of traffic fatalities. "Then you have an opportunity for cross-training among the paramedics, fire department, and towing and recovery people, for example."

To get assistance from a professional therapist or counselor, some companies have an Employee Assistance Program that offers therapy services. If not, Zimet says, finding a therapist can be as simple as going online or looking through the yellow pages.

The importance of getting help

Ginsberg stresses the importance of seeking treatment when needed. "PTSD sufferers sometimes do not feel that their doctor or therapist visits are doing much good and they don't want to go," he explains. "They also may be non-compliant with any medications they've been prescribed." When he sought disability compensation and treatment for his client, Ginsberg made his case in front of a Social Security judge, who expected to see a treatment record. "Judges expect that the claimant will put forth his best effort," says Ginsberg. "That means taking meds and going to the therapist and doctor."

Another reason that PTSD sufferers don't seek help has to do with terminology, says Maggard. "To call PTSD a disorder is a mistake," he says. "Towers go out and do this extremely important service for the community. To say they have a disorder after doing what they do is a disservice to them. I think we need to recognize that there is a limit to what any person can do."

Among the military personnel with whom he works, Maggard notes that adapting to danger saves lives on the battlefield. But if a soldier or sailor departs the combat zone too quickly or before the battle is over, he continues to have the same reactions that made him effective on the battlefield. If the situation remains unresolved, the symptoms persist.

One thing that helps PTSD sufferers, says Maggard, is to help other people who have PTSD or some other problem. "The empowerment of being able to overcome someone else's danger helps you sleep better the next night," he explains.

"After seeing so much damage and destruction that they can't tolerate any more," says Maggard, "one of the best things for a tower is to move to another level of response to the danger." This is similar to a pilot project Maggard is helping develop at Navy Medical Center Portsmouth. Working with IA's — individual augmentees— whom the Navy sends to support Army and Marine units in the field, Maggard and others at NMCP are bringing post-deployed sailors together to train, track and support their shipmates who are going to the war zone.

"After they have been first responders, they will come home and help the next wave offirst responders," explains Maggard. "They'll provide backup for their buddies who are in still in harm's way. They mayhelp a buddy's family, or send care packages or meet them at the airport when they come home. When they help other sailors overcome the stress and danger of war, that's their way of continuing the fight, and of winning."

Sometimes overcoming the trauma of PTSD happens as a matter of circumstance. Sheffer recalls several accidents in which he was able to overcome the danger and save a life. In one instance, a woman was pinned in a car that had struck a telephone pole. "She was suffering from major internal injuries and a major laceration in the groin," says Sheffer. "She was bleeding out and needed to get out of the car and to the hospital fast, or she would die."

The fire department tried everything it could but was unable to free the woman from the car. So Sheffer came up with an idea: rig his wrecker to pull on the car, and relieve enough of the pressure so that the fire department could pull the woman out of the front passenger seat. It worked. "She lived and came by my office to say thanks," Sheffer recalls with a smile. "Those are good days. They make it all worth it."

When dealing with danger and trauma that can cause — or be the result of — Post Traumatic Stress Disorder, taking care of oneself is almost as important as recognizing the suffering that others may be going through. With regard to traffic fatalities, Sheffer says that it's important to be considerate to family and friends of the victim. To that end, he keeps all fatality vehicles as far out of sight as possible. "You have to realize that you can't undo what just happened," says Sheffer. "You're there to do a job."

Sharing traumatic experiences with co-workers, friends, family or professional counselors can go a long way in dealing with PTSD. Maggard sees PTSD as a sort of injury that's exacerbated when people isolate themselves rather than asking for help. "But the more united we are, the more common experiences we have together, the more powerful we are — and so the less danger we experience," he says.

Does time heal?

In Cedar Rapids, Iowa, Dave Beer, president of Five Seasons Auto Rebuilders, is in a unique situation: two of his sons are trained psychologists. One of those sons actually works in the shop.

During his 30 years as a tower, Beer has responded to five fatalities. The first one was a vehicular suicide. "They were all uncomfortable to deal with," he recalls. "You don't even know *how* to deal with it until you're actually put in that position." Beer adds that for him, it was initially very difficult dealing with families of accident victims. What can you say, what do you tell someone who has just lost their spouse, son or daughter? Today, having experienced several of these situations, Beer says he's better able to empathize with the families' grief.

For Beer, one thing that makes a huge difference after an accident resulting in a fatality is how the first responders deal with the body. Several years ago, during a response to a fatality on an interstate highway, Beer recalls what the first responders — many of them volunteers — did at the scene: "They surrounded the body with a blanket as they loaded the person onto a stretcher," says Beer. "They protected the person's dignity like that."

Sometimes automobile fatalities happen close to home, and the resulting trauma lasts for a long time. Three years ago, Beer and his staff were in the middle of a typical workday when they received some horrifying news: the dead motorist in a nearby vehicle accident turned out to be the girlfriend of one of Beer's sons. She was killed on the highway on her way home after her last day of college studies.

"It was the worst situation that could possibly happen," recalls Beer. All of Beer's employees were friendly with his son's girlfriend because she had assisted in the shop from time to time. "She was part of our crew without officially being part of our crew," says Beer. "She was an absolute delight."

The aftermath of the woman's death affected everyone in Beer's 30-year-old company. "It literally shut our business down for two weeks," says Beer. "We could hardly cope with that. It's a situation that I don't think anybody can deal with."

Beer didn't bring in professional counselors, but he did the next best thing: he slowed down operations to allow people to grieve. "You just have to give yourself time," he says. "It took us probably a good year to get to the point where we could function at full capacity again."

Military veteran, tow truck driver

Atlanta attorney Jonathan Ginsberg represented a Vietnam veteran who was unable to keep his stateside job as a tow truck driver. The reason? PTSD symptoms made it nearly impossible for the tower to interact effectively with his customers and fellow towers.

Ginsberg went to court to get disability support for his client. "Generally judges accept PTSD as a legitimate cause of disability," explains Ginsberg. "They will want to see some trauma — combat duty, sexual abuse, those kinds of things — and consistent treatment with compliance of treatment recommendations."

According to Ginsberg, the Social Security Administration — which oversees disability payments to qualifying veterans — defines disability as the inability to engage in substantial gainful activity because of a medically determinable condition or conditions that have lasted — or are expected to last — 12 consecutive months, or result in death. "The emphasis therefore is on whether a claimant can reliably perform even a simple, entry-level, sedentary job," says Ginsberg.

For his tow truck-driving client, Ginsberg collected data supporting the Social Security criteria for an anxiety disorder, which is how the government classifies PTSD. "My client›s condition results in such an erosion of his functional capacity to work that he would not be a reliable worker."

Social Security disability uses a system of work credits. "Unlike retirement Social Security," says Ginsberg, "disability looks to the 10-year period prior to the alleged onset date." To be fully insured, adds Ginsberg, a claimant must have 20 credits out of the past 40 quarters (work five out of last 10 years). One credit is worth approximately $1,000. "When a claimant works part-time, or works for a while then stops over a period of years, he may run out of credits and thus won't qualify for Social Security Disability Insurance (SSDI)."

Jack the Therapy Dog

At G&S Service, Inc., of Johnston, Iowa, one of the employees isn't tall enough to drive, nor is he able to hook up a wheel lift to a disabled vehicle. But according to Glen Mikel, who owns the shop, this tiny member of his staff earns his paycheck every day. He's a dog named Jack.

Jack is, of course, a Jack Russell Terrier. When he's not riding shotgun in Mikel's truck, Jack keeps everyone in the office company. He's also a great stress reliever during a long day at work. "When our drivers come in," says Mikel, "Jack jumps in their laps and makes them pet him. It calms them down and helps them relax. It's really amazing to watch."

However, Jack is more than just an office mascot and ride-along buddy. Aside from his naturally friendly nature, there's another reason why Jack is so good with people: he's a certified Therapy Dog.

Six years ago, Mikel posted to a Web site for people interested in rescuing Jack Russell Terriers that had been abandoned or saved from neglectful or abusive owners. "Pretty soon I got an e-mail back from the head of the rescue organization," recalls Mikel. "They thought they had a dog that would fit me." At noon on Memorial Day of that year, the rescue organization's staff brought a Jack Russell Terrier to Mikel's home. It was important to test whether Mikel and the dog would get along with each other.

When Mikel rolled up in his truck and got out, he wasn't sure what would happen. At that moment, he says, "The dog broke away from the rescue people and ran to me. He adopted me on the spot!"

Peppy and vocal, Jack became a fixture at Mikel's towing firm. "He's a very loyal companion," says Mikel, who relies on Jack for business advice as well. During recovery jobs when a customer rides in the cab, Mikel lets Jack do the talking. "Jack is a very good judge of character. If he sits in the customer's lap and lets them pet him, then I know they're okay people," notes Mikel. "But if Jack stays away from a customer, then I know I need to watch them — and collect my money up front."

At the time, Mikel and his wifeSusan wanted to certify her Jack Russell Terrier, Annie, as a therapy dog. The test, conducted by Therapy Dogs International, would determine whether Annie was capable of providing companionship during periodic visits to hospitals, nursing homes, and other organizations where a friendly pet could make a world of difference to someone in need. The Mikels wondered if Jack might make a good therapy dog as well. "We didn't know if a Jack Russell Terrier could be trained to do anything like that," says Mikel, because the breed is known for being a bit, well, hyperactive.

On the day of the test, "Jack and Annie both passed with flying colors," recalls Mikel. Coincidentally, Mikel's next-door neighbor, who works to rehabilitate injured and physically handicapped children, mentioned that local care organizations were looking for small dogs to be used for therapeutic purposes. Soon thereafter, Jack became a regular fixture at local nursing homes and at ChildServe, an organization that assists children who have special health care needs.

At ChildServe, Jack helps children exercise their extremities by petting him, throwing balls for him to retrieve, and other activities. In addition, Jack is helpful with speech therapy because he's trained to respond to verbal commands. "Tell him to do something, and he'll do it," says Mikel. Jack works with children as young as six months old and adults up through 25 years of age.

Although he doesn't wear a cell phone, Jack is on duty seven days a week. "He's always on call with ChildServe," Mikel says. "So whenever someone needs us, we go. It's kind of like the towing business." Although Jack might not realize how many lives he improves on a daily basis, Mikel and his towing staff are well aware of how a little love from a caring pet can make the difference. "Even when we've had a hard day," says Mikel, "Jack gives us something to care about."

Towman Down!

Jason Cooke and Jarrid Mikel were two of thousands of towers across the nation, dedicated to keeping the roadways clear and safe, working hard at the jobs they loved. But in a split second, a runaway snatch block and an out-of-control vehicle would knock both Cooke and Mikel out of commission — almost permanently.

October 1, 2006 — a clear, sunny day in North Carolina. On U.S. Highway 117, a two-lane blacktop stretching for 115 miles between the cities of Wilmington and Wilson, a construction team was working on widening the highway. Suddenly their excavator plummeted into a sinkhole on the side of the road.

Thirty minutes later, Jason Cooke pulled his tow truck to a careful stop near the sinkhole. He surveyed the scene in front of him. The excavator — which weighed twice as much as Cooke's 50-ton wrecker — was drenched in mud, its left track buried in a pool of muck.

Two more trucks from Phillip's Towing in Fayetteville — 60- and 75-ton rotators — stopped alongside Cooke's vehicle, joining a 30-ton wrecker from another company that was already on scene. The towers spent the next half hour planning the recovery of the excavator, ensuring that the job would be done safely.

After the towers completed the rigging, they gave the excavator a hard pull, to no avail. "The machine wasn't moving," recalls Cooke, "so we changed the positions of the trucks and re-rigged everything."

Cooke attached four lines on the driver's side and one line on the passenger side. Another line was fastened 18 to 20 inches behind him. As Cooke began to tighten up the rigging, his equipment suddenly failed him.

"A brand-new 5/8" alloy chain broke," he recalls, " and a 12-ton snatch block came flying off the machine and hit me in the left leg." Cooke was thrown 30 feet from his truck and landed hard in the middle of the highway.

The other members of the recovery team, including Roland Russ and Cooke's boss Phillip McCorquodale, rushed over to Cooke's crumpled body. His leg was bleeding all over the pavement; his femur (the thigh bone) was cracked and sticking out. The towers cut through Cooke's pants to get to the wound, then pulled off his belt and sliced it into a makeshift tourniquet. After wrapping the belt around Cooke's damaged leg, Russ continued to provide first aid until the paramedics finally arrived.

The EMTs did their best to stabilize Cooke, then rushed him by ambulance to Duplin General Hospital in nearby Kenansville. "While this was going on," says Cooke, "Phillip made a phone call and got a helicopter in the air." McCorquodale had grown up in the area and knew that Duplin General would be unable to handle this type of trauma case, so he arranged for a medevac chopper to transport Cooke somewhere else. As the ambulance carrying Cooke pulled into Duplin General, the helicopter was landing nearby.

Cooke was immediately airlifted to Pitt County Memorial Hospital in Greenville. McCorquodale and Stewart Sealy arrived as Cooke was rushed into the emergency room. "When I arrived at Pitt Memorial, I was still in shock," remembers Cooke.

With his parents and fellow towers mounting a round-the-clock vigil, Cooke underwent surgery at 5 A.M. on October 2nd. "The doctors put a rod and six screws through my femur," says Cooke. "I had to have eight and a half pints of blood because I had lost so much after the accident."

Fortunately the surgery went smoothly, and Cooke spent the next 16 days under observation in the trauma unit at Pitt Memorial. His doctor then released him and he was sent home in an ambulance.

For Cooke, the struggle was just beginning. He was unable to bend his leg more than 22 degrees. His mother did what she could to make him comfortable, but the emotional and psychological trauma of the accident and its aftermath weighed heavily on the 27-year-old tower. "I was very, very down and out," says Cooke. In the blink of an eye, everything had changed. "Here I was, doing what I wanted, coming and going as I pleased. We had the best equipment money can buy. This was not supposed to happen to us."

Cooke spent 92 days on his back. When he wasn't in bed, he worked with a physical therapist, desperately trying to regain a full range of motion in his battered leg. "It was a painful experience," says Cooke. "I had all these thoughts of not being able to walk again, not being able to play with my little girl again."

But he refused to throw in the towel — not only for the sake of his three-year-old daughter but also for the job he loved. Cooke kept at it, exercising his leg, suffering through bouts of excruciating pain. He used a walker to get around the house. Thanksgiving and Christmas came and went with Cooke unable to enjoy either holiday. His birthday passed him by.

Then, finally, some progress. "Sometime around the end of January I was able to move around a little bit better on my walker," Cooke recalls. "And I started using crutches for the first time." McCorquodale dropped by and drove Cooke to the office. Cooke hadn't been there since the accident three months before. "It was kind of hard, but I was glad to be back," says Cooke.

Soon after, with the encouragement of his family and fellow towers, Cooke returned to work as the operations manager for the Wilmington office of Phillip's Towing. He continued his rehabilitation, working with a physical therapist three times a week.

But in April, Cooke suffered a setback. "There was a two-and-a-half inch area of my femur that was shattered and didn't grow back together," he says. "So on April 2nd I had to have a second surgery." Doctors replaced the original rod in Cooke's leg and swapped out the original six screws with a dozen new ones. Finally, by June, Cooke was able to return to work.

Then came the most important part of his recovery: Cooke got back in his truck. McCorquodale issued him a new 2007 Kenworth rollback with automatic transmission. Slowly but surely, Cooke was getting back where he belonged. "I still have limitations as far as my leg is concerned," he says, "but I do work calls as I'm physically able."

Although the physical scars are healing gradually, the psychological trauma from the accident is another hurdle that Cooke must overcome. "There are some things we do as far as tractor trailers are concerned where we have to pull out the chains. When we do that," he says, "I get butterflies in my stomach."

But, adds Cooke, the support of his supervisor and fellow towers makes a huge difference in his day-to-day recovery. "It's a family atmosphere. Philip has done some things I don't think anybody else in his position would have done." McCorquodale took care of Cooke's financial obligations until worker's compensation insurance started to pay the bills. "He and his family bent over backwards to make sure that I was okay," says Cooke.

McCorquodale also gave Cooke the necessary push when it was needed. "There was a time when I was down and out and didn't even want to talk on the phone," recalls Cooke. "Phillip would call my mom to see if I needed anything. Sometimes he would call me and say, 'Jason, get your butt out of bed. We're going out today.'" Because of all the support he has received, Cooke considers himself fortunate to be part of McCorquodale's company.

Reflecting on the incident that almost cost him his leg, Cooke has one thought in mind: "We buy the best equipment, the best trucks, the best of everything for the wreckers in our business," he says. "It becomes second nature that if we have the best, then nothing's going to happen. But it does. Just because you have the best that money can buy, people still get hurt." Although these types of incidents happen every day, "you never expect it to happen to you," he adds.

And what are Cooke's plans for the future? Once his leg allows it, "I want to go back to driving the heavy wrecker."

Perhaps the only towers who can truly empathize with Cooke are others who have been through similar circumstances. Twelve hundred miles northwest of Cooke's office is the town of Des Moines, Iowa — the home of G&S Service/I-80 Towing, Inc. There, three years ago, owner Glen Mikel saw one of his employees through a horrible accident — except in this case, the victim was Mikel's own son.

On a bitterly cold winter morning, Jarrid Mikel responded to a call from a state patrol car. A Ford van had broken down and was resting next to the jersey barrier on the East 14th Street bridge, part of Interstate 80 in central Iowa. It was 5 A.M. and the asphalt was thick with ice and snow.

Mikel turned his collar to the cold and hooked the van up to the wheel lift on his wrecker. He tied down the left front tire and began working with the right front wheel.

Suddenly a pickup truck, barreling down the highway at a rapid clip, spun out of control on the bridge. The pickup flew into the disabled van, hitting Mikel with enough force to throw the 20-year-old tower underneath his own truck.

Though badly hurt, Mikel was able to pull out his cell phone and make a call. "He's on his Nextel hollering at one of my drivers for help," recalls Glen Mikel, Jarrid's father. "I was out of town on a heavy recovery call. When they told me what had happened, I turned my truck around and came right back."

When Glen Mikel arrived at the accident site, the Department of Transportation had blocked off a traffic lane and was pouring salt and sand on the icy roadway for traction. An ambulance had rolled up, joining the police cruiser already on scene. The EMTs were preparing to move Jarrid to the ambulance. Glen helped carry his son's stretcher over the jersey barrier, rolled it into the ambulance, and watched as the doors closed. The EMTs triggered the siren and the ambulance moved slowly away, its tires crunching on the frozen asphalt.

Jarrid was being transported to the nearby Iowa Methodist Medical Center. As he made his way to the hospital, Glen received a phone call from his wife, who was already there. "They've just sent the chaplain in to

Jarrid's room," she said. Glen's mood, already glum, took another hit. "To me that meant Jarrid was a goner," recalls Glen.

Fortunately it was a false alarm. Glen's wife Susan called back and said that rather than delivering last rites, the chaplain was actually functioning as an advocate for trauma patients. He had been sent into Jarrid's room to counsel the injured tower, not to say goodbye.

Glen parked at the hospital and found Jarrid's surgeon. "He told me that Jarrid had broken both tibias and his left fibia," remembers Glen. "His pelvis was cracked, he had nicked his spleen, and some of his teeth were chipped." The surgical staff inserted titanium rods into Jarrid's legs, then placed him in traction, where he remained for several months. Friends and family visited him constantly while he recovered in the hospital.

"He had good support," says Glen, who had the family barber come to the hospital to give Jarrid a haircut. "People would get him out of bed and push him around the hospital in his wheelchair." One day when Jarrid was out and about, one of his friends brought glow-in-the-dark stars and put them all over the walls of his hospital room. When Jarrid went to sleep that night, he turned out the light and the star stickers lit up all around the room — a warm reminder from the people who cared about him.

Concerned that his son might not walk again, Glen took a tough-love approach to the recovery process. "I felt that it was my job to keep him pissed off and aggravated at me," says Glen, "to give him something to feed on instead of his injuries." To exercise his son's injured legs, Glen alternated placing tongue depressors on Jarrid's toes. Jarrid, feeling the wooden instrument on his feet, would wriggle his toes in response. Glen also brought his family's two therapy dogs — specially trained to help those in recovery — into the hospital to visit Jarrid.

As the weeks went on, Jarrid was determined to get back on his feet, and his father encouraged him in that direction. "Don't listen to what the doctors tell you," Glen would say to his son. "You just keep working and you do it. There isn't anything you can't do. You just keep trying until you get what you want."

When he was released to return home, Jarrid began physical therapy. "The worker's compensation people made our house handicapped-accessible for him," says Glen. But the bone marrow that had been injected into one of his legs didn't take, and he had to return to the hospital for another marrow transplant. The doctors weren't too hopeful about his chances; his legs were so badly damaged that they didn't think he would walk under his own power again.

Jarrid, though discouraged, wasn't about to give up. "He wasn't about to sit at home in a wheelchair," says Glen.

As part of his recovery, Jarrid was outfitted with removable casts. Before Glen realized it, his son had taken his casts off and was driving around town. "He just kept going," says Glen. "When we first got him home, he was driving around in a blizzard in the Explorer, helping out the other towers where he could. He was always involved in towing and didn't want to be away from it."

Meanwhile Glen fought a different battle for his son. The company that supplied worker's compensation insurance for Mikel and his employees burned through their cash reserves and decided to stop insuring tow companies due to the risk involved. "That put us out looking for worker's compensation insurance because of a claim that wasn't our fault," says Glen. "Being down a man and having to pay high worker's compensation rates was a real inconvenience to us."

Soon Glen found a smaller company that was willing to continue the insurance. Unfortunately, the problem still persisted: Even though the original insurer was eventually reimbursed for the claim by the party responsible for the accident, "We as towers are still stuck with high rates even though it wasn't something we did," explains Glen.

When it looked like Jarrid's worker's compensation would be unable to cover the costs of his recovery, the members of Tow411.net conducted a pledge drive that netted more than $1500. When he found out that insurance would offset his medical costs after all, Jarrid asked that the money collected in his name be donated to the Survivor Fund administered by the Towing & Recovery Hall of Fame & Museum in Chattanooga, Tenn.

Looking back, what happened to Jarrid was an unfortunate, but preventable, accident, caused by a careless driver who ignored what was right in front of him. "The guy in the pickup was driving too fast for the weather conditions," says Glen. "The pickup came screaming down the road and lost control. Jarrid didn't have a clue that it was going to happen."

Today, Jarrid's legs are still scarred from the accident, but he's back on the road, running heavy-duty operations for G&S Service/I-80 Towing. Despite some tough times, he refuses to let the accident slow him down. "He was certified by the Towing & Recovery Association of America at age 14," says Glen. "He recently completed heavy-duty and rotator school with Wes Wilburn."

And Jarrid is just shy of 23 years old. "He continues to work every day," says Glen. "He knows he's lucky to be around."

Dangerous, Deadly and Bizarre: Towers Attacked, Part 1

Although towing companies do a lot of planning ahead — to put together their drivers' work schedules, to execute a recovery operation efficiently, to be as safe as possible — sometimes a seemingly normal workday can be interrupted by unforeseen or bizarre circumstances out on the road. And sometimes — despite hours of training and preparation — there's little or nothing a tower can do about it.

Whether a tower is conducting a recovery, a repo job, or is moving an illegally-parked vehicle, sometimes the owner of the vehicle reacts badly, putting the tower's life in jeopardy. Tow truck drivers have been shot at, stabbed, set on fire, and had their trucks vandalized. Sometimes towers have even been murdered. While these incidents are rare, they're worth looking at — if only to be aware of what might could happen on one of those days when something — or some*one* — goes haywire.

51

Dangerous

Tempers can flare when a vehicle is towed against the owner's wishes. In September 2008 a woman in Portland, Ore., was so upset at the tower who was about to remove her illegally parked car that she refused to pay the $150 release fee. Then she tried to set the tow truck on fire.

The tower, who was in his truck at the time, called 911, jumped out of the cab with an extinguisher and put out the fire. "Police found the charred remains of a fast-food bag and wrappers in the back of the truck, and a one-gallon gas can about two feet from the blaze," reported *The Oregonian* newspaper. In an attempt to avoid the police, the woman modified her hairstyle and changed her clothes, but her disguise didn't work and she ended up in jail later that day.

Even church parking lots aren't immune to bizarre incidents. In one instance a vehicle owner in Concord, N.H., came upon a tow truck driver who was preparing to tow his car, which he'd left in a no-parking zone overnight. The vehicle owner came after the tow truck driver, the men fought and the tow truck driver was knocked off the bed of his truck. He landed on the pavement and fractured his skull.

While it's unfortunate — and shocking — that some vehicle owners get downright violent about seeing their property being carted away, some towers believe that the country's current economic problems are triggering even more frustration than usual. After almost 1,200 vehicles were towed during bad weather in St. Paul, Minn., one tower found the windows smashed on his only truck. "It had to be related to the snow emergency, because this truck has sat here for months," Clarence Kempke of CNS Services Towing told KAAL-TV. "No damage to it. They call a snow emergency and this is what I get. It's very frustrating. Now I have to spend excess money."

Several other tow truck drivers were attacked as they went about their duties. "We don't know if it has to do with the economy — people getting a little more upset when they have to pay that $300 to get their car out," remarked a police spokesman.

Lack of money and the resulting stress can cause people to act in strange ways — even to the point of brandishing a weapon in front of a tow truck driver. Ed Pavel, vice president of the Illinois Recovery

Association, told the *Chicago Tribune* that he'd seen an increase in the number of repo jobs since June 2008. Each of those repossessions has the potential for triggering an altercation between towers and vehicle owners.

"It cranks up the emotions of these people," said Pavel. "They're angry. And we're the ones who bear the brunt of their emotions when we come to their door." To protect themselves, some recovery operators are putting video cameras in the their trucks.

Case in point: Professional Recovery Services, based in Palatine, Ill., tried to repo an SUV and a Cadillac from a home in Hoffman Estates, a suburb of Chicago. Instead the three-person recovery team found themselves facing a man who was pointing a gun at them. The towers, who had already hooked the SUV to their truck, drove away. As they did, the man fired at them multiple times. Fortunately none of the towers was hurt.

Disputes between vehicle owners and the towers who remove illegally parked vehicles came to a head in Bluffton, a small town in southern Georgia. Preston Oates, the owner of Pro Tow, was about to move a vehicle out of a mobile home park when the people inside the nearby home came out and argued with him. Then one of the people pulled a knife and stabbed Oates.

"Oates said the knife went about 10 inches into his body, narrowly missing a kidney and other organs," reported the *Hilton Head Island Packet.* "He was taken to Memorial Health University Medical Center in Savannah, where he underwent surgery over the weekend."

It turned out that the residents were locked in a battle with the management of the mobile home park. The latter had taken an aggressive stance against vehicles "improperly parked on the streets and in front yards." Already sheriff's deputies had to calm a protest down after approximately 15 vehicles were towed or booted. And Oates' company, Pro Tow, had generated its own share of controversy over its perceived aggressiveness at removing vehicles.

Oates had taken to carrying a gun to protect himself and had already been involved in an incident that summer where he shot at three men while attempting to repossess a vehicle. Oates reported that the three men advanced on him carrying a handgun, sticks and beer bottles. After the confrontation was over, police arrested Oates. His reaction to both incidents? "On July 16, I defended myself and ended up in jail," Oates told a reporter. "On Friday, I didn't defend myself and ended up in the hospital. What am I supposed to do?"

Unfortunately, sometimes the bullets fired by disgruntled people found their mark. "I felt the wind from the bullet come right by my head," said tower Jesse Vasquez of Phoenix, Ariz. "He almost took me away from my kids." Vasquez had just been shot three times by an irate customer. He had finished towing the young man's car after it was involved in an accident. While he was running the man's credit card, Vasquez glanced up and saw something shocking.

"I looked in the mirror, in my rear view mirror, and he's pointing a gun right at me," said Vasquez. "He starts unloading and the second shot hits me." The shooter hit Vasquez twice in the lower back and once in the lower leg. Neighbors came to Vasquez' aid as the shooter barricaded himself inside his house. He surrendered to police soon afterward.

Why did a customer who had turned over his credit card to pay for a $154 tow suddenly pull a gun and fire at the tow truck driver? Vasquez wasn't sure. "He didn't give me any indication he was mad. If anything, he said he was gonna pay the bill." The shooter's explanation was nothing short of bizarre: he told police that Vasquez was too slow and had stolen the keys to the vehicle. Even if it were true, why would the customer feel compelled to fire a hail of bullets at the tow truck driver?

Deadly

Angry or disturbed people sometimes strike out against towers — like Jesse Vasquez — who were just trying to do their jobs. But sometimes the situation gets worse: sometimes towers are murdered on the job. The police have solved a number of these crimes; other cases still remain open.

On March 24th of this year, tower Jose Fernandez moved through the parking lot of The Outpost, a 20-acre complex of student apartments in San Antonio, Texas. He was checking to make sure that the vehicles displayed the required parking permits.

Sometime before 3 a.m., someone shot Fernandez four times — "including in the back of the head, chest, and legs," reported local TV station WOAI. Hearing the gunshots, some of the residents ran into the parking lot. One of them saw a gray truck driving out of the complex. "It's especially unsettling after many of them heard gunshots at this same apartment complex on Friday," explained TV reporter Kristina de Leon. "Police are trying to see if the shootings are connected."

Liz Johnson, vice president of Alamo City Recovery, the firm that employed Fernandez, announced that the company had set up a memorial fund, asking for donations from the public. "As many of you have heard, one of our drivers ... was shot and killed early Tuesday morning while walking in an apartment community looking for a parking violator.... Our thoughts and prayers are with the family of our driver, Jose Fernandez, during this terrible time," said Johnson.

Police eventually charged a graduate student from the University of Texas at San Antonio with the murder. Strangely, the student phoned 911 after the shooting, claiming to be named "Ben Wade" — a character in the movie "3:10 to Yuma," which the student had just purchased at a local Target department store — and threatened to shoot a witness if the police didn't call back within five minutes.

Though the student didn't follow through on his threat, police eventually linked him to a bank robbery and another shooting. He was arrested and held on a $2 million bond.

Two hundred miles west in the city of Houston, Mario Jove, a tow truck driver for Spring Branch Towing, was growing increasingly dissatisfied with his job. As the *Houston Chronicle* reported, "At first, the good money seemed to be a fair trade for the stress and long hours required to do the job. But as time wore on, Jove decided towing the cars of disgruntled people in a high-crime area was not worth the pay, his family members said." He had spent six months on the job and decided it wasn't for him.

Not a problem — many people try out certain jobs to determine whether they're a good fit. But before he could switch careers, Jove was gunned down in cold blood.

On September 28, 2008, Jove came upon an illegally parked car in an apartment complex and prepared to tow it away. It was a little after 5 p.m. Two men were sitting in the car, drinking. After Jove snapped a photo for documentation, one of the men in the car jumped out and fired a weapon at Jove, hitting the tower in the back repeatedly. Jove collapsed on the ground as the shooter jumped back into the car and drove off. The one item that could help police solve the case — the photo that Jove took — wasn't accessible because something happened to the camera when Jove dropped it after being shot.

"It's not one of those cases where it's a bad guy shooting a bad guy," Houston Detective Ray Leon said, adding that Jove was "a hardworking guy trying to take care of his family."

Meanwhile on the west coast, Performance Towing in Merced, Calif., was missing one of the vehicles in its fleet. Someone stole the company's white GMC 1500 pickup on a Monday night in November 2008. Later that evening Randall Armendariz, Sr., one of the drivers at Performance Towing, saw the missing vehicle on the street and confronted the thief, who pulled a gun and shot Armendariz in the head. Police pronounced the tower, a father of four, dead at the scene. The stolen truck was left with the engine running and the door open. Armendariz was a "good, likable" person, recalled one of his co-workers. "We went on a lot of trips together getting cars."

Sometimes pure coincidence resulted in a tower's inadvertent death. A tow truck driver was starting a right-hand turn in a Phoenix, Ariz., neighborhood when a single bullet suddenly shattered the windshield of the tow truck and hit him.

Nearby a man ran out of his house and saw the tower lying on the ground. The truck was rolling toward a nearby house. The man jumped into the truck and slammed on the brakes, then checked the tow truck driver. But the tower was already dead.

Where had the bullet come from? It turned out that man who helped the tower was the same person who had shot him. He had been cleaning a rifle inside his one-story house when the gun went off by accident. The bullet sliced through the blinds, cracked the window, and screamed toward the tow truck, killing the driver.

... And just plain bizarre

By contrast, some incidents are just plain bizarre. The *North Shore Outlook*, a newspaper covering the Vancouver area, introduced tower

Mitchell Martin to its readers in this way: "He's repossessed a Hells Angels enforcer's prized Dodge Viper and Mercedes, both in the same week, had dirty diapers hurled at his head and been kicked in the face while operating his tow truck."

Obviously Martin had dealt with a variety of situations during his time on the road. But nothing could have prepared him for what happened when he tried to remove an illegally parked SUV from the underground parking lot at a local medical center. The owner of the SUV, a pregnant woman, accosted Martin as he hooked up her vehicle to his wrecker. Several more pregnant women got involved as well.

The *Outlook* described what happened next: "Outnumbered, Martin decided it was best to lock himself inside the truck and call the [police]. Even the young son of one of the rampaging women joined in with a verbal uppercut: 'F*** you Mr. Tow Truck.'"

Martin sat in his cab, watching as the women threw his equipment off his truck, broke the side mirror and made scratches in the paint. Although Martin survived the ordeal, he remembered it as the worst incident he had ever encountered in his decade-long career in the towing industry.

Although towers know to stay vigilant and safe while out on the road, there's only so much they can do to guard themselves against the sudden appearance of a gun or knife at incident scene. Hopefully, knowing what some towers have experienced — towers who were threatened, injured or, shockingly, murdered — will help others survive similar incidents in the future.

Fighting Back:
Towers Attacked, Part 2

The previous chapter featured part one of our two-part look at towers in danger — recovery jobs complicated by circumstance, repo and impound tows interrupted by furious vehicle owners, and just plain bizarre occurrences that towers would never forget. The stories are shocking, revealing and sometimes outlandish. But each of them provides us with insight into what towers have experienced on the job — and, just maybe, gives us ideas about how to respond to similar situations.

This time around we'll take a look at some additional incidents, then delve into ways that towers can deal with similar circumstances — or, if the situation requires it, how to fight back.

Narrow escapes

Any tower who's been on the job for a while has enough stories to fill a book. Mitchell Martin, owner of Mitchell's Towing in North Vancouver, British Columbia, Canada, has had his share of run-ins with angry customers. "I have had dirty diapers throw at my head, I was jumped and beaten up by two guys in an alley, and my back window has been blown out during a repo," he says.

Mix surprise, anger and frustration during a recovery operation, and sometimes towers barely escape with their lives. Late on a Friday night, police in Portland, Ore., pulled over a driver and charged him with a DUI. His wife, who was also apparently drunk, arrived on scene a short while later, looked around, then departed. The tow truck arrived to take away the husband's vehicle, so the police officer on scene decided to chase after the wife on a suspected DUI.

While the cop was out searching for her, the wife came back and approached the tower, telling him that if he took away her husband's car she would go get a weapon. Then she went home, later returning with "what appeared to be a gun," according to local TV station KGW.

At that point the tower decided that his personal safety was more important than getting killed over a simple impound job. He drove away, leaving behind the car he was supposed to take away. Later that day the police visited the wife at her home, but she refused to come out. Forty-five minutes later, she finally gave herself up. Like her husband, she was charged with a DUI.

Sometimes towers have to defend themselves with words, their fists or, in extreme cases, a weapon. When a tower fired a gun at a vehicle owner near a nightclub in January 2006, was it a case of self-defense — or attempted murder?

Donald Montanez, owner of Private Property Commercial Impound in Tampa, Fla., was supervising multiple impound tows outside of the Sugar Shack Club. One vehicle owner, told that Montanez's employees had moved his car to a staging area, went with two brothers and a friend to get his car back.

At the staging lot, the vehicle owner retrieved in his car and drove directly toward Montanez. Fearing for his life, Montanez pulled out a gun and shot the vehicle owner. According to the *Tampa Bay Times*, "Defense attorney Jeffrey G. Brown argued that Montanez had a fraction of a second to act and fired a .40-caliber pistol to try to disable the vehicle as [the driver] drove at an accelerated speed toward Montanez and an employee."

The case went to trial that May. Montanez's legal team tried to get the murder charge dismissed, while the prosecutor held that Montanez and his employees were towing cars that turned out to be legally parked.

Lost and runaway wreckers

Some stories of towers in trouble are truly amazing. A July 2007 headline in the *New York Daily News* no doubt raised some eyebrows: "Swallowed Tow Truck Finally Pulled from Crater." An underground steam pipe had exploded, blowing a 15-by-25-foot crater into Lexington Avenue in Manhattan. As the asphalt crumbled underneath vehicle traffic, a tow truck fell into the crater. The driver and his passenger — whose car he was towing — both went to the hospital with burn injuries resulting from the 400-degree eruption of steam.

Later, workers rolled a nine-story crane over the crater and pulled the tow truck to the edge. After that, the *Daily News* reported, "the vehicle was then raised up again — this time more than four stories into the air — and carried about 30 feet away from the hole."

Consolidated Edison (Con Ed) hauled the debris — including the tow truck and other vehicles caught in the blast — to a facility in Queens where it would be scoured by investigators. The faulty steam pipe was 84 years old and apparently exploded because cold water somehow seeped inside it.

For the tow truck driver, Gregory McCullough, every day after the incident was marked with physical pain. "Putting on a shirt takes me 10 minutes," he told NBC's *Today* show in November 2007. After the truck fell into the crater, McCullough told his passenger that they should make a run for it or risk being boiled alive by the steam. They both jumped out of the truck and dashed for safety. "[McCullough] ran through the scalding steam, fell on the pavement, rolling in agony, got up, ran some more," reported Mike Celizic of *Today*. "He ran into a building, begging for help, and he remembers people looking at him as if he were an alien and backing away from him, horrified at the vision of a man whose skin had melted off most of his body. Finally, others poured water on him and called 911."

As part of his recovery, doctors put McCullough in a medically induced coma that lasted two months. And his passenger that day? McCullough's quick thinking saved her life as well.

On the flip side, inexperienced or inattentive towers can create a lot of damage all by themselves. In March 2009 the driver of a Ford F550 flatbed accidentally sideswiped a sedan in the town of Brookfield, Ill. As the sedan crashed into a nearby van, the tow truck driver lost control of his wrecker and smashed through the windows of Slager's, a small tavern nearby. "The impact sent bricks, car parts, window frames, tables, chairs and glass flying across the front of the bar," reported the *Riverside Brookfield Landmark*.

Fortunately everyone involved — including the drivers of the tow truck and the sedan — survived the ordeal with only minor injuries. "One of the paramedics told me to buy a lottery ticket," said a surprised man who was seated inside the pub during the incident. "I sort of heard a swishing sound and thought, 'What is that?' Then I went flying and landed on the floor sitting up. I didn't know if a bomb went off or it was a gas explosion."

The tow truck driver, employed by a local company for barely two months, was fired. His truck was totaled in the incident, and the case is currently under review.

A similar incident in Rome, Ga., occurred in the opposite way: This time a vehicle driver hit a tow truck, sending the wrecker speeding into the Magic Wand Car Wash nearby. After banging up some equipment at the car wash, the tow truck crossed oncoming traffic lanes, smacked a power pole, and drove through the front wall of the World Hi Fi Home Store. Fortunately, because the accident happened early in the morning, no one inside the store was injured.

In Detroit Lakes, Minn., a runaway tow truck cost one tower a limb. Michael Smith, owner of Lakes County Towing, underwent several surgeries after being injured as he helped prepare a county disaster drill in September 2008. A school bus posing as an overturned camper rolled down an embankment and smashed into Smith's empty tow truck. As his truck slid down the hill, Smith jumped into the cab in an attempt to stop his truck. But he made it only halfway into the cab. The truck slid past a tree, slamming the door on Smith, breaking his pelvis and damaging his leg. His leg was later amputated above the knee.

"He is with us and for that I am praying every moment," his wife wrote in the *Park Rapids Enterprise*. "There have been steps forward and just as many backwards but Mike is sustaining."

Being careful, fighting back

While freak accidents and acts of nature are out of the tower's control, incidents involving angry customers can, in many cases, be solved peacefully — or prevented altogether. But if a tower inadvertently finds himself or herself in the middle of an altercation with a customer, there are several ways to fight back.

Jesse DeGraeve, owner of Anytime Towing in Traverse City, Mich., recalls some of the ways that he and his employees have dealt with these kinds of sticky situations: "Usually from what I have seen, people are the most agitated when they come to pick their car up," he says. "When we first opened up, I would bend over backwards to come in after hours to let people into a car or to pick up a car. After dealing with a few shady characters and having to call the police once, we ended that." Now DeGraeve only lets people pick up cars during office hours. "This way there is more than one person around," he explains. "Irate customers are much less likely to cause problems with more than one person there."

When on scene, Mitchell Martin sometimes faces angry vehicle owners who approach him in the middle of an impound or repo job. If Martin is inside his truck, rolling away with the vehicle, and someone comes running up alongside him, Martin usually locks the doors and rolls the passenger window down. Martin then points to the passenger window. "For whatever reason it always works," he says. "They go to that side and then they're not directly in my space or within striking distance."

On the other hand, if Martin is outside his truck and busy hooking up a vehicle, he takes a different approach. "I find that most people who catch you in the act are aggressive at first," he says, recommending that towers keep calm and avoid raising their voices or "flexing their chests." Remember, says Martin, "You're the professional. No amount of money is worth going home to your family injured."

When dealing with possible altercations, DeGraeve notes that he's been lucky. "We haven't had any problems where we have had to fight physically with any customers or where any customers have attacked a driver," he says. "But I tell our drivers that if they have a strange feeling about a call or if something doesn't feel right, then pass on the call." If his driver is already at the call and something happens, DeGraeve instructs his employees to call the police first, then do whatever they need to do to get to a safe spot.

Martin provides a few tips on how to deal with an angry vehicle owner and keep that anger from bubbling over into a fistfight — or worse. First, explain why the vehicle is being towed. "Make sure you have the most information possible before arriving," urges Martin. "You never want to be caught and not know why you're doing the job."

Hooking up the vehicle as soon as possible can give the tower an advantage if the vehicle owner seems ready to go overboard. "Get the vehicle lifted in the air," says Martin. "People are easier to talk to when they see their prized possession — whether it's a Pinto or an Aston Martin — in the air." Easy, fast and widely accepted multiple methods of payment can also speed the process along.

Sometimes, to be extra safe, towers carry their own weapons. "Michigan is a state where concealed weapons permits are available," says DeGraeve, noting that a lot of the tow truck drivers in his town have these types of permits. But is it the best way to keep yourself from getting hurt? Martin is concerned that people who carry a weapon might be more likely to use it. "I don't think anything more than pepper or bear spray is needed," he says. "Your intentions are never to fight. If there are a lot of people at the scene, try to pull the owner aside. Try making it sound like a deal — $40 now but $105 later at the yard." Calm, sensible negotiation with an irate customer might mean the difference between a quick tow and suffering an injury on the job.

For towing companies that want to protect themselves financially against physical harm, insurance is available. "One of the coverages important to the industry pays a benefit in the event of felonious assault," says Ralph Weber, founder of Route Three Life Health Disability, Inc., a Paso Robles, Calif.-based firm that provides insurance and financial services to the towing industry. Fortunately there have been few if any payouts for such coverage. "To be honest, that I have not heard of any specific incidences of that happening," says Weber.

When it comes to dealing with angry vehicle owners, Martin picks his battles carefully: "Nobody really wants to fight," he says. "Most people you can talk down. I'm not a big guy so I use what God gave me." His advice? "Treat them with respect, and you will be respected. Your ability to make a quick decision is a must," he adds. "Every situation is different and requires a calm individual."

What's In Your Truck?

There's nothing better than a "fully equipped" tow truck. But what exactly does "fully equipped" mean? For many towers, having the proper gear onboard is critical to getting the job done. Like many government agencies the Utah Department of Transportation, for example, requires certified tow trucks to carry equipment like portable lights, wheel ties, a scoop shovel, broom, safety vests and fire extinguishers.

Depending on the towing company, gear like this is supplemented with a variety of tools for operating in certain areas and climates. "We have booster packs with 1700 cca (cold cranking amps), several different recovery straps and chains, unlock kits and AAA literature, towing manuals as well as the almost required GPS navigation systems," says Mitchell Martin, owner of Mitchell's Towing in North Vancouver, British Columbia, Canada. "We also have bike and tailor packages, onboard air compressors as well as an assortment of hand tools to pull drive shafts."

That's an impressive toolbox. But what about *inside* the cab? When a tower spends so much time on the road, what does he or she keep inside the truck to make the job go more smoothly? What items can a tower not live without, keeping him company as he travels from job to job?

Previously we told you the story of Glen Mikel, owner of G&S Service, Inc., in Des Moines, Iowa. When out on the road, Mikel often shared his cab with Jack, a Jack Russell Terrier who was trained as a certified therapy dog. In addition to working with children and adults at hospitals and nursing homes, Jack served as Mikel's partner when dealing with customers. "Jack is a very good judge of character," Mikel said at the time. "If he sits in the customer's lap and lets them pet him, then I know they're okay people. But if Jack stays away from a customer, then I know I need to watch them — and collect my money up front."

Other towers might not have a dog to talk to in their truck, but the items they carry are just as valuable. "I have a laptop with internet access," says Nick Schade, director of operations for Tony's Wrecker Service in Lousville, Ky. "I have three cameras, a cell phone, duffel bag with personal items and personal protective equipment that can be easily transferred from truck to truck." Schade also carries a CB radio and a power inverter to convert DC current to AC.

A clean business

Just as important as the equipment towers carry in their trucks is the fact that they want their vehicles to be clear of dirt and debris. "I try to keep my truck and my employees' trucksclean,without a bunch of clutter in the cab," says Jesse DeGraeve, owner of Anytime Towing in Traverse City, Mich. "I find that customers appreciate the trucks being clean."

Towers note that although they keep certain necessary items in their trucks, much of the other equipment they carry is there to help their customers. "Most of the stuff in our trucks is for the convenience of the driver and customer," says Martin, adding that the truck cabs are a "mini office" of sorts, containing credit card and debit machines along with pens, pads and staplers.

"In our trucks,our business card is in a card holder right in front of the customer on the dash," says Mike Patellis of Alpha Towing in Marietta, Ga. Every effort is made to ensure a clean-looking cab, says Patellis: "We have a 'no smoking' decal in front of the passenger seat, no air fresheners, no greasy seats." Kevin Farthing, owner of Waffco Heavy

Duty Towing in Lake Station, Ind., agrees: "We try to keep our trucks clean and free of debris," he says.

Preparing for the unexpected

A good selection of safety equipment can make all the difference. Martin carries vests, coveralls, jack stands, aluminum jacks and a first aid kit onboard his vehicles. Al Gregg, operations supervisor for Dakota Towing Service in Brookings, S.D., stays prepared for the weather. "I carry a duffel bag full of gloves and hats," he says. "After all, it's South Dakota!"

Gregg also carries a first aid kit wherever he goes. "This is a dangerous business," he explains. Another important piece of equipment in his truck? A set of field glasses — binoculars — to identify recoveries that are supposed to be close to a roadway.

You never know when you might get stuck somewhere overnight. Mike Eskew of Barnett's Towing in Tucson, Ariz., takes no chances. In his cab he keeps a fresh roll of toilet tissue, extra flashlight batteries, a phone charger — "and one change of clothes for that unscheduled overnighter," he says.

"Nothing is worse than staying overnight on a job, showering in the hotel and then having to put on dirty clothes to finish the job the next day," says Eskew. "I would almost liken that to kissing your mother-in-law. Yuck."

Special equipment

Mixed in with all of the technical equipment are some creature comforts. "All the trucks have a GPS, flashlight, lock-out kit, gloves, and a good stereo — something that plays MP3s," says DeGraeve. "These are all things we need to do our jobs with the exception of the stereo. The stereo just makes life a little more pleasant when you're riding around in a truck all day."

Martin urges all drivers to make sure they give their trucks a thorough run-through before hitting the road. "I've seen a lot of drivers go to a job without looking through their trucks," he explains. "After arrival they realize, 'I don't have this, I don't have that.'" After he started his own business, Martin took these lessons to heart. "Too often fuel, time and effort is wasted with lazy drivers," he says. "Nothing is more important that to have the right equipment to do the job right the first time."

I Have a Question!

The phone rang in Jeff Watson's office. He picked up the receiver and put it to his ear. A harried voice on the other end of the line asked a very serious question: *Do you have tow trucks?*

Watson, owner of Avilla Motor Works, Inc., in Avilla, Ind., gets this question a lot. And he always answers "Yes," very politely. Then the potential customer asks the typical follow-up question: *How much would you charge me?* Watson gets a fix on the type of vehicle, quotes his rate, hops in his truck and motors out to the incident site.

When he gets there, sometimes he wishes he had asked a few more questions. "I show up and it turns out the car, truck or tractor is upside down or 300 feet off the road or stuck to the frame in mud," says Watson. "You do what you have to do, and then you hand them the bill — only to hear them start pissing and moaning about what the job cost them." Watson's response: "Look, I didn't build it, buy it or break it," he patiently explains.

Towers are used to answering a myriad of questions from their customers. Some of those questions have been asked a million times, on

71

every job, every day. Other questions come out of left field. During one recovery job, Mike Patellis, owner of Alpha Towing, Inc., in Marietta, Ga., pulled his wrecker to a stop and jumped out. The customer who had called him was waiting with a question: *Are you the fella who came out here last time?*

We asked people across the country for their lists of top questions, and here's what they told us.

The basics

Let's start with answers from local governments, which often put together helpful information for residents whose vehicles have been towed without their consent. For example, in Arlington County, Virginia, a one-page brochure addresses basic questions like the following: *If my car has been towed, what do I do to find it? Can I be towed from the parking lot of a closed business? Why would a business care about parking in the lot when it's closed? If I return before the tow truck removes my car, do I still have to pay?*

Sometimes tow companies provide a list of frequently asked questions to potential customers. Chico Towing in Bremerton, Wash., shares information about towing and impound services on its Web site. The first question on the list is at the top of most towers' greatest hits: *If I call for a tow, how long will it take for your truck to reach me?*

"We try to reach all our customers within 30 to 45 minutes," answers the company Web site. "This is typically a reasonable expectation. However, during peak times it may take 30 minutes or more extra. In adverse weather conditions, we always try to reach people exposed to the elements before those safely indoors."

That's about the same amount of time that Jesse DeGraeve, owner of Anytime Towing in Traverse City, Mich., tells people when he's asked the same question. "Usually people are looking for a quick response time," DeGraeve explains. "We shoot for within 30 to 45 minutes depending on the location of the call and how busy we are."

Some customers are more savvy than others when it comes to the technical requirements for towing a vehicle. Patellis has been asked if he has flatbed trucks in his vehicle fleet. In Brookings, S.D., Al Gregg, operations supervisor for Dakota Towing Service, recalls being queried by the owner of a car regarding a front-end tow. *Do you need to put the car in neutral?* asked the customer.

On the scene

Then there's the issue of payment. "Every customer wants to know how much our services are going to cost them to get the job done," says DeGraeve. "We have a set rate schedule that we go off to give them an accurate figure." Nick Schade, director of operations for Tony's Wrecker Service in Louisville, Ky., notes that one of the top questions he's asked is, *What is it going to cost?* — immediately followed by, *Why does it cost so much?* Mike Eskew of Barnett's Towing in Tucson, Ariz., gets a variation on the theme: *How cheap are you?* Eskew finds it humorous. "I've been called a lot of things," he says, "but cheap isn't one of them."

When the job is done, Kevin Farthing, owner of Waffco Heavy Duty Towing in Lake Station, Ind., sometimes has to debate his rate with an irate customer. *Do you take my motor club card?* "Ninety-nine percent of the time this answer is no," says Farthing. "Why so much?" asked one victim of a police-ordered tow. "My cousin got busted for the same thing last week in the next town over," said the customer, "and it only cost half as much." Farthing shakes his head at the memory. "You just can't fix stupid, can you?"

Other questions are more specific. *Can you bill my insurance company or me?* "No to both," answers Eskew. In South Dakota, Al Gregg often gets a basic question — *Who do I make the check out to?* — but also has to deal with young people who ask him, *Can you charge it to my parents?*

Then there are the towing jobs that end with an angry vehicle owner berating the tow truck driver for hitching up private property without their consent. *Why was my car towed and why is it so expensive?* "This is usually from the person whose car was involuntarily towed or impounded by the police, illegally parked, or abandoned and the property owner called to have it removed," explains DeGraeve. In that type of situation, says DeGraeve, he and his staff try to explain the reason for the tow, as well as the reasons for the pricing. "Sometimes people are understanding about it," he says. "Other times, things can get interesting."

At the end of the job

Once everything's hooked up and the customer understands what he or she is paying, what's next? Time to get out of there. Is someone picking up the customer? Or is the customer accompanying the vehicle to its destination?

Although towers might take a customer along in the cab, the tow truck isn't a shuttle bus. Mike Eskew had to explain this to a customer who asked, *Can my four passengers ride in your truck?* Sometimes, though, the question is an easy one: *Can you drop me off by my house on the way to the garage?*

As with all good customer service, towers do their best to answer whatever questions are tossed their way. Whether they've heard the question a million times or are thrown a curveball, towers take care of the customer as best they can.

But sometimes even the most resourceful tower can be left speechless. Take this instance, when Patellis picked up a ringing phone in his office one day. He took down the details, answered the customer's standard queries about time and money — and then wasn't sure what to say to the next question. Love must have been in the air that day, because the customer asked Patellis in all seriousness: *Can you send that girl driver out?*

Heavy Metal:
Tractor-Trailer Recovery, Then and Now

There's always a bit of truth in every cliché, and one in particular — "the bigger they are, the harder they fall" — could serve as the theme of the heavy recovery operator. Today more than ever, rescuing tractor-trailers requires expertise and versatility unique to the heavy recovery "road warriors."

Bill Robertson of United Road Towing, Inc., is a 45-year veteran of the industry. After building and selling his own towing firm — "like many others, we grew one customer at a time, one truck at a time," he says — Robertson now serves as a consultant, traveling across the United States to each of United Road Towing's 10 branches. "I check safety procedures, review driving habits and train drivers, mostly in heavy-duty operations," says Robertson.

When working on the West Coast, Robertson is teamed with safety/compliance manager Paul Johnston, who works out of the company's Ontario, Calif., location. Johnston's responsibilities include follow-up inspections, maintaining the company's standardized safety training program, and keeping photographic records. According to Johnston, United Road Towing requires its operators to sponsor regular safety meetings to review federal and state towing requirements.

During his many years of supervising heavy towing operations, Robertson has seen many technological changes take place. "What we're towing today is a lot more fragile," he notes. "We have ABS brake systems, computer-controlled engines, and fairings instead of those big old tough bumpers we used to have." Some of the technology is quite delicate. "Sealed drive shafts require no lubrication, but if you break them it might cost you $500 to $800 to repair because you've damaged the integrity of the shaft."

Many modern trailers are equipped with soft or fiberglass sides. In addition, yesterday's common 40-foot trailer has grown to 53 feet, which can create a less stable, flimsier trailer — and consequently a tougher job for the tow operator. Kevin Farthing of Waffco Towing & Recovery in Lake Station, Ind., notes that the longer trailers "have composite walls, fiberglass roofs and very thin floor decking. If you're not careful, these characteristics can mean disaster during something as simple as winching a trailer out of the mud."

Farthing adds to the list of improvements over the years: aerodynamic design, lower oil pans, air dams, side cab air foils and automatic transmissions. "All of these things require today's towman to be more experienced, educated, and given better equipment," says Farthing. "It's no longer the old days when we used a Holmes 750 and a bumper pad."

Bill Robertson agrees. "Before you'd take an ex-road tractor trailer with half a million miles on it and then set a tow truck body on it." Using practical experience and consumer feedback, today's manufacturers continue to fine-tune their products, focusing on the features that heavy recovery operators need.

"They're building us equipment to fit our industry much better," says Robertson. Wheelbases are longer, up to 330 inches. Road differentials have been boosted from 34,000 pounds into the 46,000-48,000-pound range. Robertson praises manufacturers for improved communication with customers, noting that tow companies can now order trucks from the factory with the required cross-members, air tanks, compressors, solid gearing and transmissions.

Even with such up-to-date equipment, recovery operations are only as good as the tow operator behind the wheel. "We strive to put not one more scratch than what we started with," says Robertson, who laments the fact that a number of towers are performing heavy recoveries without proper training or experience. Kevin Farthing recalls several jobs where avoidable mistakes damaged the tractor-trailers being recovered, including "strapping trailers during uprights or winch-outs and not paying attention to the delicate middles." He also notes that some towers fail to use air cushions to stabilize long or flimsy trailers.

Brian Bolus of Minuteman Towing & Repairs, Inc., which operates six locations across northeast and central Pennsylvania, echoes Farthing's concerns. "Improper rigging can be the cause of significant additional damage to the unit you're recovering," says Bolus. "Take the time to rig the wrecked units properly and don't cut corners as it will only increase the recovery time in the long run." If something doesn't look or feel right, says Bolus, "stop and access the situation and re-hook if necessary."

What else can towers do to avoid these types of mistakes? "Talk to your peers and get their input," recommends Farthing. Relying on other towing companies for help is also an effective solution. "Call another company to help you, one that has the equipment you might need to accomplish the task."

While taking the time to rig the job properly is sound advice, the reality of the road can sometimes make it difficult for even the best towers to perform efficient recoveries. Law enforcement and local government agencies need the roads cleared quickly to get traffic moving again — a requirement that can sometimes be at odds with the tower's job. "Some police officials and departments of transportation don't understand how much time it can take to recover a unit safely and properly without creating additional damage," says Farthing. "It's a challenge to appease all parties involved and also do our job to the best of our ability."

With different parties' needs bumping against each other, "it pushes the towers harder," says Bill Robertson, who notes that useful tools like air cushions are not as predominant as before because of how fast the wrecks need to be cleared. In some cases offloading the wrecked trailer is required — not a popular event with law enforcement officials who want to get traffic flowing after an incident.

Robertson notes that relationships between towers and law enforcement agencies have improved over time: "After being exposed to a number of tractor-trailer accidents, police officers gain a lot of knowledge. They can almost take a look at an overturned tractor-trailer and know how long it'll take to clean up, which really helps when we're trying to take the proper time and attention during a heavy recovery operation." Doing the job right is critical, says Robertson. "If you deliver a customer's equipment to him in three pieces, he's not going to be happy."

Given all of the changes on the road and in the factory, heavy towers stress the importance of proper training — both to initiate new drivers into the field and to keep them fresh through follow-up courses. "It's a bigger challenge for the drivers and equipment than ever before," notes Robertson. "You have to have more training, to show the drivers how to handle all of it."

Heavy recovery operators are always faced with danger as well as the prospect of damage when working particularly tricky jobs. "The liability thatwe are always exposed to can be greatly reduced withwell-trained drivers," notes Brian Bolus. Bolus says that purchasing late-model equipment, rather than using band-aids to keep out-of-date towing vehicles on the road, greatly increases the safety factor and provides for better training. "Unfortunately, this aspect is overlooked in many towing companies."

"Our worst problem is in taking shortcuts," says Bill Robertson. "Some towers don't really have enough training in heavy recovery work. It's fairly easy to get into this industry and onto a rotation list with local law enforcement agencies." However, strong local standards can help the situation. In California, for example, towers are required to show experience, number of trucks, number of years in business, what types of training they provide, and other data prior to hitting the road. In addition, operators are subject to background checks.

At United Road Towing, Robertson and other supervisors push what they label "recurrent" training for their operators. "We have it going constantly," he says. "No matter how long you've been in this business, if you don't learn something new every day, you're missing out on something out there." Robertson also recommends taking advantage of low-cost, high-quality training offered by state associations in addition to courses sponsored by private firms.

Paul Johnston notes that he and Robertson perform many drive-a-longs with their drivers. "We use those occasions as both teaching and learning tools," says Johnston. "We never fail to learn something new from our drivers that we can pass along to others."

In addition to practical, on-the-road education, Johnston says that many things have changed with regard to driver proficiency training. "In years past we used the 'foggy mirror' test: We'd put a mirror under a driver's nose, and if he fogged it up indicating he was alive, we would put him in a tow truck. No legitimate towing and recovery operation today can use that as a standard," says Johnston. "We now talk about orientation training, recurrent training, certification training and on-the-job training and experience." Johnston regards his company's investment in safety programs and training as keys to ensuring "a healthier bottom line."

Kevin Farthing takes that idea one step further, recommending that in the future the federal government create a standardized towing and recovery course "for any and all towers participating in traffic incident management." Farthing feels that this level of oversight would ensure that all tow operators are prepared for whatever happens on the road. "Too many tow companies and tow operators buy a truck, get insurance, then go to local law enforcement and request to be placed on the rotation list" without first ensuring that they've received the proper training for the job. Robertson agrees, noting that a number of companies don't make sure that their operators are ready before they begin recovery operations.

The dangers have increased over the years. In the past, "we were younger, dumber, and had more fun with it," notes Bill Robertson. "We had to work harder because we didn't have all of today's nice hydraulic equipment, air cushions, all of the new technology." Robertson feels that present-day heavy recovery is more stressful on the operator. "There's more traffic to deal with, fewer breakdown lanes on freeways if you're disabled, have a flat, or the vehicle has quit running." Many breakdown lanes have been converted to carpool lanes, making it harder for disabled vehicles to find a spot off the main road.

With increased traffic on American roads these days, heavy operators need to maintain visual awareness while working a recovery. "One of our biggest challenges is in staying safe on the highway," says Kevin Farthing. "Never assume that the motoring public can see you or will steer clear of you."

United Road Towing recently lost one of its own in Phoenix, Arizona, when a hit-and-run driver slammed into him as he was preparing a vehicle for a tow. Supervisors at United's local branch were tracking its operators using a GPS system. "When dispatch noticed that he wasn't moving on the GPS," recalls Bill Robertson, "they sent someone out to check on him. They found him on the side of the road. He didn't make it." The driver who killed him may never be found.

The sad recounting of stories like these are a grim reminder of the challenges faced by heavy operators every day. For owners of towing companies, losing one of their own is a tragedy — even more so because it's difficult to find good drivers. In the job market, transportation companies compete directly with heavy recovery outfits for the best employees. "All of these companies are looking for the same type of person, whether they're Schneider, Swift, J.B. Hunt, or a towing company," notes Robertson.

Although transportation and towing companies dip into the same talent pool for employees, Robertson says that candidates in the heavy recovery industry have a tougher job description. "The biggest challenges for a cross-country transportation driver might be reading a map or GPS and backing into a tight warehouse dock at the destination," says Robertson. For towers who recover tractor-trailers, the job requires additional expertise: "We might have to hook a 40-foot truck onto the front of a tractor-trailer, maneuver it through city streets, and then back the damaged trailer into a loading dock. It takes some practice."

Heavy recovery operators need to be even more vigilant when a tanker truck carrying chemicals overturns on the highway, spilling hazardous material (HAZMAT) onto the road. Properly trained HAZMAT specialists can contain the spill and deal with any environmental and physical consequences. "HAZMAT has a tremendous amount of short- and long-term liabilities and risk that most towers don't have the training for," says Brian Bolus. To protect themselves, towers should consider preemptive action including HAZMAT-specific certifications, equipment, medical surveillance programs and insurance. All of this preparation is fairly new to the industry, says Bill Robertson. "Years ago, we didn't have a clue. If it wasn't on fire, we thought it was all right." Training with expert organizations like fire departments improved the towers' response. "For example," notes Robertson, "we learned to find the bill of lading first, so we knew what the HAZMAT actually was before getting anywhere near it."

The bill of lading is just one of the multiple pieces of paperwork that heavy recovery operators deal with every day. Insurance issues require another set of records entirely. According to Brian Bolus, heavy towing has changed over the years due to escalating insurance and equipment costs. The lack of industry-wide standards in equipment and training make it difficult for insurance companies to track prices and rates, which can vary widely from company to company.

"Insurance and trucking companies use prices from one towing company as a benchmark for another company without regard to demographics or individual circumstances," says Bolus. "They paint our industry with a broad brush," which is problematic since rates also vary by geographic region.

Sharing rate information is one solution to the confusion that occurs with insurance claims. "We as towers need to bridge the gap," says Bolus. "Trucking and insurance companies are often skeptical about large recovery invoices because they've been burned in the past by towing companies who charge more than they should for a particular situation." Farthing notes that as trucking and insurance firms gain knowledge, tow companies that fail to share truthful information will increasingly find themselves under heavy scrutiny. "Nowadays you're paid for your knowledge and skill, not for how long you take to finish the task," he says.

Good records help simplify the sometimes difficult insurance process. "The key is to document everything and send a well-prepared invoice that describes the entire recovery," recommends Bolus. An accompanying package of photographs can be e-mailed to provide visual support to the recovery records. "In the past we didn't have detailed billing so that the insurance adjuster could do his job properly," remembers Bill Robertson. "Nowadays the billing is more detailed, so we have stronger lines of communication among truckers, towers and the insurance industry."

Robertson recommends that towing companies treat insurance companies as return customers. "You want to treat them fairly," he says. "They're a big part of your customer base." Helpful towers are invaluable to the insurer's claim process. "I have yet to see an insurance company refuse to pay a fair bill," says Robertson.

While handling insurance issues is a critical component of the job, everything starts with the quality of the tow itself. As in any industry, there are good and bad companies doing business with customers, some of whom get fleeced. "Some towers take all of their equipment to a scene, don't use it all and then charge for it being there," laments Kevin Farthing.

Brian Bolus agrees. "The good and bad of our industry is that the best companies don't always get the call," he says. This is sometimes due to the structure of local rotation lists. Some companies on the list fail to invest in the proper equipment, leading to delays during recovery operations. "When recoveries drag on, the highways back up," notes Bolus, adding that customers have the right to know exactly how a towing company is charging them for a job.

How can the heavy towing industry serve its customers better? Farthing stresses the importance of using properly sized equipment. "We can't be lazy or uneducated," he says. "For example, recently one company picked up a Freightliner bobtail from us. To tow the bobtail, they used a single-axle wrecker with a 108-inch wheelbase — much too undersized for the job. To add insult to injury, the driver didn't go to the axle but used the trick of dropping a chain through the pull hooks and towing on them." These kinds of shortcuts damage equipment and reputations, says Farthing.

For the larger heavy towing firms, establishing a centralized organization can be an effective way to standardize the quality of service. United Road Towing is one example of a company that owns all of its branches nationwide. While some owners and operators might disagree with this type of consolidation, Bill Robertson believes that the industry can only benefit. "I don't think this business model ever took business away from anyone," he says. "In fact, I think it really helped."

Robertson points to his company's stringent set of guidelines, from uniforms to training to safety procedures. "If we purchase a towing firm that isn't quite up to par, we work to improve it. Then the competition

82

responds by stepping up. In the end, everyone's business improves, and the customers receive better service."

"In this competitive industry, sometimes we're tempted to throw the next guy under the wheels of the bus," says Brian Bolus. "We need to work together and put the egos aside. That way we'll all benefit, and our industry as a whole will have a brighter future." Bill Robertson praises heavy recovery operators, whose dedication and unique expertise make all the difference: "Once people join the towing and recovery business, they usually stay. It gets in their blood. Every day out there is different."

A House with an Engine in it:
Luxury Coach Recovery

On a bright sunny day several years ago, a retired husband and wife were driving their luxury coach — a Winnebago Vectra they had purchased just two weeks before — on an open stretch of the westbound I-90 in northwest Washington. Behind the motor home the couple was towing a tiny Suzuki Samurai. Tired from the long drive, the husband dozed off behind the wheel. The huge 17-ton vehicle veered onto the center median strip and struck a row of fiberglass reflective posts.

The shotgun-like sounds of shattering fiberglass immediately woke up the husband, who panicked and jerked the steering wheel to the right. As the motor home started to fishtail, the husband oversteered in the opposite direction, and the right rear tire rolled off its bead. The aluminum wheel caught the pavement and the motor home pitched on its side. The enormous vehicle spun down the asphalt as the Samurai behind it turned upside down and whipsawed back and forth. The two vehicles gradually skidded to a halt in the middle of the freeway.

Call them what you will — coaches, campers, caravans, motor homes, recreational vehicles (RVs) — these gigantic homes-on-wheels are the ultimate in mobile luxury. But when one of these big vehicles breaks down or is involved in an accident, the luxury coach becomes a huge challenge for the tow operator. Many luxury coaches are built on truck chassis, but recovering an RV is nothing like recovering a truck.

The high value and heavy weight of many coaches requires a tow operator with special experience and a high risk threshold. Consequently, many towers understandably shy away from working with luxury coaches. "They can be a pain to load or tow," says Al Gregg of Dakota Service and Repair in Brookings, S.D. The challenge can be daunting, says "Stormin'" Norman Stenberg, a 15-year industry veteran in Entiat, Wash., 90 miles east of Seattle. "Ninety percent of the time you get out there and it's, 'Hmm ... How are we going to do this?" he says. "That's scary when you're looking at a motor home worth $500,000 to $1 million."

So what makes the luxury coach a tough job to tackle? "It's the way they're built," says Stenberg. Adds Gregg, "Most of these coaches are 'pushers' (rear-wheel drive with dead axles to bear the load) which have short little shafts in the rear." In the past, tow operators could pick up a motor home using the frame or a cross-member, but today's air suspension and airbag systems create serious clearance issues, requiring the tower to reach deep underneath the vehicle to find a hook-up spot. Difficult-to-remove drivelines and axle covers, along with inconveniently located leveling jacks, can create additional difficulties for the tower. "You need extra-long equipment to do it," says Stenberg, who typically uses a two-stage wheel lift in his recovery operations. "We move a lot of RVs on Landoll-type trailers or with heavy-duty tow units using an L-arm type of lift with wheel lift grids," says Bill Robertson, founder of Bill and Wag's Towing in Los Angeles.

For tow operators, "it all gets down to, is the risk worth the amount of return?'" says Robertson, who notes that many RV owners have tow coverage through a motor club or other membership association, and that the organizations sponsoring these programs are constantly searching for vendors who will charge lower rates. "But tow companies often refuse to tow these fragile, expensive units while charging automobile or even tractor-trailer rates," he adds.

Success or failure in recovering luxury coaches is ultimately dependent on the skill and experience of the tow operator. "Even with all the equipment you can get," says Robertson, "you need a very good operator with experience and good common sense." As with other vehicles, technological and stylistic changes in the last several decades have made the job of towing a luxury coach much more difficult. Many modern motor homes dispense with the traditional straight axle in favor of an independent front suspension. Today's coaches also feature titanium A-arm suspensions, electrically operated steps, and low-mounted exhaust systems, to name a few.

The other end of the tow job — pulling the vehicle into its destination — presents problems as well. Robertson notes that towing onto driveways can be a difficult task with a luxury coach, as the massive weight and low underbody clearance can scrape the vehicle along the ground, on both the front and rear ends. And don't forget the foliage: Dangling tree limbs create additional hazards for towers, as some RVs extend as high as 14 feet into the air. So-called "basement unit" RVs offer lots of storage space underneath the floor, which increases the height of the vehicle.

Every coach is a brand-new challenge, says Stenberg. "We have to figure out how to hook up each individual one. A lot of times we have problems because there's not enough room, and we have to move things out of the way to hook up."

As with any recovery job, hooking up in the right places is critical. "Towing operators need to be knowledgeable about where they can and can't pick up a motor home," notes Doug Tolberg, president of Powerhouse Coach in Idaho Falls, Idaho. "A wheel lift is almost dictated these days because chassis aren't designed to have that weight anywhere but on the wheels." Some sort of instruction manual would be helpful, says Norman Stenberg. "The American Automobile Association and General Motors, for example, have books that show you how to hook up and tow a car. Motor home dealers have nothing like that."

Like many tow company owners, Stenberg supplements the basic certification provided by organizations like the Towing and Recovery Association of America with local hands-on instruction. Put simply:

no experience, no towing. "In my company," says Stenberg, "you don't do anything until you have 30 hours on the road with me. I personally train all of my employees." In addition, Stenberg praises the Commercial Driver's License (CDL) program offered by individual states.

Training and experience were key during recovery operations for the luxury coach that toppled over on the I-90 in Washington. Kevin Johnson of D&M Motors and Towing, based in Ellensburg, supervised the tow. Fortunately, the retired couple that owned the motor home had escaped the accident without injury by kicking out the passenger-side windshield and scrambling onto the asphalt. The RV had skidded to a stop on its right side, while the Suzuki Samurai it had been towing lay upside down, blocking the remainder of the two-lane roadway.

Johnson and his team responded with a Holmes 1801 and a Vulcan 1616 to recover the motor home, and a Holmes 1201 to tow the Suzuki. The crippled luxury coach had come to rest in the fast lane with its tires pointed toward the shoulder. The shoulder, protected by a steel guardrail, dropped off into a soft dirt embankment that rose from a small stream in the middle of the highway. Blocked by the guardrail, Johnson realized that he would be unable to perform a conventional recovery.

Johnson parked his Holmes 1801 parallel to the motor home and just three inches away from the guardrail. After positioning his truck's stiff leg for a side pull, Johnson placed the Vulcan on the opposite side of the road, next to the center embankment. "We used two guardrail posts as winch anchors," he explains. "We connected in front, up over the frame, then back over the front axle. Then we winched the vehicle into an upright position." At first the luxury coach threatened to slide on its side, so Johnson inserted a steel chock under the flat tire and wheel.

Careful planning and placement of equipment resulted in a successful motor home recovery. "You have to pull awfully hard when you're using the frame to upright something," says Johnson, "because you don't have much leverage — maybe two feet from the center of the vehicle — to pivot it up." By connecting to the frame, Johnson avoided any further damage to the motor home.

The possibility of doing additional damage to a crippled luxury coach makes many tow operators uneasy, with good reason. With some motor homes valued into the million-dollar range, one tiny error can be devastating to a tower. "One scratch to a coach with an expensive mural or a custom clear coat paint job can cost thousands of dollars to fix," says Bill Robertson.

Norman Sternberg recalls a very delicate recovery job: "One time I went out to pick up a motor home. I got out there and I'm looking at a brand-new Monarch." (One of Monarch's newest vehicles boasts a gross weight of 22,000 pounds, a 242-inch wheelbase, a length of nearly 37 feet and a height of 12 feet.) "I walked up to the vehicle," Stenberg continues, "and the price tag was still on it — $500,000. That brings up a lot of liability issues."

To protect himself and his company, Stenberg carries a liability insurance policy worth $1 million. He cautions that tow operators who strike a bump in the road risk fracturing the skin of the luxury coach. "I know of one company that was towing just a regular motor home, not even one of the big coaches. They hit a bump really hard and broke the skin of the motor home. That accident cost the tow company $46,000."

The cleanup of hazardous materials is also a consideration during recovery operations with motor homes. During the I-90 incident in which a sleepy driver sent his luxury coach into a long skid on the highway, the damaged vehicle soaked the road with engine oil. Kevin Johnson thought about shaking gravel or sand on the liquid to soak it up, but instead carefully avoided the spill. "Our local law enforcement and our insurance company had both cautioned us about the presence of HAZMAT at an accident site. They said, 'Let the Department of Transportation handle that. You're not in the HAZMAT business.'" So Johnson worked around the spill.

Later, when the RV owners' insurance firm contacted Johnson about the accident, "they expected to declare the vehicle as totaled," he remembers. "I said, 'When you come look at it, you might be surprised at how good a condition it's in." The insurance company thought that the tow chain and straps might have caused some injury to the vehicle, but were surprised to find no additional damage to the coach or chassis. Johnson and his team had performed a solid, safe tow operation. Instead of being shuttled off to the junkyard, the motor home was re-towed by Johnson to a repair facility, and was back on the road soon after.

How can manufacturers design luxury coaches that are friendlier to the tow operator? Doug Tolbert of Powerhouse Coach has one answer. Tolbert brings a unique perspective to the table: he's a former tow operator who now builds custom motor homes for a living. His experiences with towing motor homes inspired him to move into the production arena. "I had a towing company and an auto body shop," he recalls. "I saw the problems with production coaches. So I built one for my own personal use." Local customers were impressed with Tolbert's work and asked him to build RVs to their specifications. What began as a side interest gradually developed into a full-time business.

Tolbert uses Class 8 semi truck chassis — "million-mile chassis," as he calls them — in the construction of his luxury coaches. "The typical motor home is underpowered and overloaded," he says. "If you look in a manufacturer's brochure, you'll find that many of these RVs are back-heavy even before you load water, fuel, and personal belongings into the vehicle. Consequently that chassis is being overworked all of the time."

During his time as a tow operator, Tolbert saw a lot of overheated motor homes whose engines and transmissions died while on the road. He also noticed that many motor homes stopped running because of fairly minor problems. "Unfortunately, if an RV broke down in a rural area, the owner couldn't get it fixed there because the parts were so specialized." By building luxury coaches using a semi truck chassis, Tolbert says, basic components like a driveline U-joint or water pump hose are readily available almost anywhere.

How can towers get more comfortable with towing luxury coaches? A major part of the solution lies in building motor homes that are more accessible to tow trucks. Al Gregg notes that engineers who design luxury coaches need to take the tow operator into account when the vehicles are on the drawing board. "The manufacturers need to get together with the towing people," agrees Norman Stenberg. "It's important, because towing these coaches is risky and expensive." Stenberg notes that in north central Washington, it can cost up to $250 an hour to tow a motor home.

As Kevin Johnson says, "Diesel pushers like these motor homes were never meant to be towed, so doing recovery work on these vehicles is a big job." But he adds that sometimes the challenge is worthwhile, as with his successful rescue of the luxury coach on the I-90. "You tow cars and trucks every week. It's the more challenging recovery and tow jobs that drive our industry to improve our equipment and techniques on a constant basis."

Light Duty Towing

What's the deal with light duty? It's sometimes considered a poor cousin to medium- and heavy-duty towing operations. More complex recoveries get more attention and require bringing out the big guns to rescue trucks, tractor-trailers, buses and other large vehicles. Bringing in the heavy-duty equipment can have certain advantages for the tower, says David Lambert, president of the North American Towing Academy in Altamonte Springs, Fla. "Less wear and tear on the equipment, less rigging, and the billing may benefit both the operator and his company," he explains.

But, says Lambert, not everyone agrees with this assessment. "The abilities of light and medium-duty equipment may surprise some towers," he explains. "A tower who understands the capabilities and limitations of his equipment can perform miracles with light- and medium-duty trucks."

The gear for the job

Many towing companies stock tools to cover a variety of recoveries. Towers like Al Gregg, for example, own a mix of light to heavy-duty towing equipment. Gregg›s Dakota Towing Service, based in Brookings, S.D., was launched in 1982. Gregg prefers good used equipment and likes 5,000 or 6,000 pound lifts with "chassis to match," he says.

Gregg praises Zip's, which sells Miller equipment, as a service-oriented distributor. "There are a lot of great manufacturers of towing equipment to choose from," he says. "I personally like to buy from those companies, like Zip›s and Miller Industries, that give back to our industry. I think most of the major equipment manufacturers and distributors do just that, and each tower in a given area will support those distributors close to them."

Gregg says that towers in his area are very fortunate to have Zip's, Twin City Wrecker, Roy's Auto, Williams Wrecker, and North Central Truck & Trailer—"sales representatives who really care about us and the equipment they sell us," he says.

Over at Fast Tow Wrecker Service in Houston, Texas, current owner Charles Rash runs a company founded by his father in the 1930s. Says Rash: "My father bought a used Army truck, built a homemade rig, and went to work towing in Houston. The towing rate was $7.50 per tow and 50 cents a day for storage." Today, nearly 75 years later, Charles Rash's three sons operate the company across three locations. Rash, who also prefers Miller products, operates 30 light-duty trucks including 26 Vulcan 804s and four Jerr-Dan rollbacks.

At Bob's Garage & Towing, Inc., in Painesville, Ohio, the father-and-son team of Jay and Jared Fox oversee four full-time and four part-time drivers, plus three mechanics in the garage. The company was established in 1965 by Robert Fox as a light-duty operation with two wreckers and a two-bay auto repair shop. By the mid-1970s Fox had expanded the business to three trucks—two wreckers and a flatbed. After Jay purchased the company he updated the equipment with wheel-lift wreckers and, in early 2003, added heavy-duty towing and recovery to the menu.

Today the company runs 10 recovery vehicles that feature Century, Jerr-Dan, Vulcan and Champion equipment. "We have light, medium, and heavy-duty wreckers," says Jared Fox. "We also have flatbeds along with a skid steer loader, an incident response trailer, and trailer dollies for towing damaged trailers."

Overlooked and undervalued?

Why are light-duty towing and recovery often overlooked? "It's human nature," says Gregg. "It's like watching a young boy go down the street to deliver the newspaper or watching a silver-backed gorilla do the same task. The gorilla will get more attention, even though there are more paperboys around."

"The same is true in our industry," continues Gregg: "The heavies are more exciting. There is an adrenaline rush each time you fire to go on a heavy recovery, and it seems to become almost a spectator sport when you're out there doing your job. But if you're performing a light-duty recovery on the same stretch of highway, traffic flies by not caring if you're there or not. (And we do wish they'd care enough to slow down and move over.)"

Recent years have brought new developments to the light-duty arena. Two years ago the Roanoke, Va., municipal government tackled a local issue with light-duty towing. Residents complained about the city's system for police-requested towing services because rates varied depending on which towing companies arrived on scene. The result: different vehicles involved in the same accident were sometimes charged different rates. In the fall of 2006 the Roanoke city government reworked the system, dividing contracts into "light duty" and "medium/heavy duty" categories.

"Light-duty tows are the towing of passenger cars, minivans, and most SUVs," read the city's request for proposal. "Medium/heavy-duty tows involve the towing of delivery trucks, tractor-trailers, and other heavy-duty vehicles." The city planned to create pricing controls over light-duty tows but decided to leave medium- and heavy-duty tows to the market since "it is more difficult to create a fair pricing system for medium/heavy-duty tows."

The result? "An award was made to several towing companies for light and heavy duty," says Sharon Gentry, the purchasing manager for the city. "Two separate contracts were awarded depending on equipment. They are called on to do work on a rotating basis. The system is working very well; the tow company owners were very responsive."

In Texas, Rash says, this year marks the first time that police and private-property towers must be trained and certified according to state regulations. "That's about 50,000 trucks and drivers," he adds, "including transport trucks." In Harris County, which includes the city of Houston, Rash notes there are four million vehicle registrations. "That adds up to a lot of possible tows." As an example, he says, the city of Houston racks up over 160,000 non-consent tows annually.

Light duty vs. heavy duty

So what are the differences between David and Goliath—light- and heavy-duty towing, respectively? Rash draws the distinction this way: "Light duty is about customer service; heavy duty is more about the big 'toys.'"

On a more technical level, Al Gregg says that light-duty towing and recovery are usually done by tow trucks that are heavier than the disabled vehicle being recovered. For heavy duty it's usually the opposite. "There your casualty is usually heavier than the tow truck," he says, "oftentimes utilizing two tow trucks to perform the recovery."

In addition, says Gregg, most light-duty recoveries are accomplished on unibody cars. "If you hook low and to the high corner on the front end of the vehicle," he explains, "once you have tension on your wire rope the chances of the vehicle tipping over are very slim." On the other hand, recovering a tractor-trailer combination requires that the tow operator have complete control over the equipment and cargo being recovered.

"The main difference that we notice in light-duty towing isthatinthe lastfive to 10 years the cars have become more delicate to handle," says Jason Strickland, owner of Strickland Towing in Haven, Kan. "There are fewer places toattach chains and straps for recovery, aluminum a-arms and flimsy rear axles. Thelack of a true framemakesa correct hook-up a major safety issue." Operators must be careful when hooking up and

96

ensure they examine all possible rub points for chains and straps, he says.

Strickland also notes that the last several years have seen a proliferation of cars with pop-out tabs in bumper covers for fixed loops. He's also seen many screw-in eyelets on automobiles like the BMW, Volkswagen and Mini Cooper models. "Educating operators about the proper places to attach chains and straps has become a priority," he says.

At I-70 Towing and Recovery in Columbia, Mo., drivers use flatbeds and wheel-lift trucks for light-duty rescues. According to Jennifer Furlong, dispatcher/secretary for the company, "We use dollies on recovery vehicles that have total suspension damage in the front and back, so that all four wheels are off the ground."

In the training arena, Lambert notes that over the last several years there has been greater interest in light-duty training. As an example, he points to the Professional Wrecker Operators of Florida, Inc., headquartered in Orlando, which sponsored nine light-duty training classes in one year, compared with two for heavy-duty operators.

"Never ask a trainer if any type of training can be overemphasized," chuckles Lambert. Despite about 95 percent of all towing and recovery being light-duty operations, he says that the current emphasis on incident management means that heavy-duty operators get the limelight. "Law enforcement expects a trained operator to arrive on the scene of a major incident," says Lambert. On the other hand, he adds, it's important to remember that most incidents that close an interstate involve light cars and trucks rather than eighteen-wheelers.

In addition to being careful with standard equipment—dolleys, winches, booms, chains and snatch blocks—Ferguson notes that "winch cables are smaller and more apt to break, so being aware of your stationary obstacles to work around them so you will not break equipment and still maintain safety."

Training and cross-training

"You can't buy experience but you can train for the future," says Rash. He notes that at every recovery scene, all of the major players often have extensive training: the fire department, police, EMTs, EMS, and even the media. Tow truck operators should be just as prepared. "Sometimes a tow truck driver pulls up in a $50,000-plus truck and the only training he has is how to drive and maybe make out his ticket," says Rash. "If you are lucky he won't kill or injure someone during the recovery or wind up on the Wall of the Fallen."

Training is critical when an accident shuts down a major highway, says Lambert. "When there are hundreds of cars and trucks backing up on the interstate, burning gas, polluting the environment and the level of road rage is rising, side streets are getting crowded. Goods and services, packages and letters, and people are delayed," he says. "Because of the financial and environmental impact, it's important that all the operators be trained, not just heavy-duty ones."

What about cross-training between light and heavy-duty operators? Learning all types of towing operations is beneficial to both the tower and the company for which he or she works, says Gregg. "As a small operator, I try to have all of my employees familiar with both because usually a heavy recovery or major accident will require that most of my staff will be going out," he explains. "A cross-trained employee is a more valuable asset. At the same time, he is more marketable if opportunity presents itself. If I were an employee I would want to cross-train, just to broaden my possibility of working for a larger variety of employers."

Lambert agrees, noting that training in light-duty towing doesn't necessarily prepare an operator for heavy-duty operations. To be more effective as a tow operator, Lambert urges that heavy-duty operators build a solid foundation in light-duty recovery. "A good light-duty recovery program will include the basics, like equipment ratings, stabilizing the truck, effects of snatch blocks, and calculating resistance," he explains. "Once you understand the basics, it's easier to move on to heavy."

According to Lambert, approaching the training in this manner helps bridge the gap between light and heavy towing techniques. "We start learning in elementary school and then progressing to high school," he explains. "This is similar." As for medium- vice heavy-duty towing, he says that there is little difference between the two arenas.

Overall, says Rash, training is the most important aspect of running a towing operation. "I drove a truck for 25 years and have been to over 250,000 incident scenes," he says. If the worst happens, lawsuits can be costly, so be prepared, he says. "When you are defending a lawsuit over your liability limits and go to court, you'd better have that driver's training certificate with you."

"Advanced equipment and a lot of excellent trainers have really advanced our industry," notes Gregg. "You don't want to spend the rest of your life thinking 'what if?' or 'why didn't I?'," says Rash. "Get involved in training."

Interesting developments

Old hands and rookies can all benefit from light-duty training. At Avilla Motor Works, Inc., in Avilla, Ind., owner Jeff Watson rang up an expert when he set up his new towing service two years ago. "Since we are newbies in towing," he says, "we sought out Wes Wilburn to help with our training needs—and we have a lot!" Watson has been in the repair business for 11 years and runs a six-bay shop. He's starting slowly with his new towing division and currently operates two trucks. One is a 2004 International Harvester 4300 rollback, while the other is a 1998 IH 4700 with a Chevron LMD 512 bed. The rollback features wireless remote-controlled winches manufactured by the British firm Lodar Wireless Solutions.

Watson's rollback truck is also equipped with a directional recovery unit supplied by American Enterprises in Oregon, Ohio. "The advantage to our unit is that you can pull 180 degrees, right to left, all the way around the back," says Dave Jaeger, who owns the company. "All of the other units available are side-pullers." Jaeger notes that while other units include 100 feet of cable, the American Enterprises product has a 160-foot cable with a wireless remote control.

Gregg makes a quick list of his light-duty equipment: self-loading wheel lifts, Go-Jacks, self-loading dollies, skates and arrow sticks, to name a few. "Advanced equipment and a lot of excellent trainers have really advanced our industry," he says.

According to Mark Sawyers, the current president of Recovery Solutions, "Without a doubt, the most important development is the self-loading wheel lift invented by Dave Craze and Calvin Russthrough their company Dynamic Manufacturing." The self-loading wheel lift made all types of light-duty tows safer, says Sawyers, including repossessions, private property and public safety tows.

Adds Sawyers, "I'm biased, of course, but I bought the self-loading wheel lift from Recovery Solutions for years, long before I bought the company."

"The amount of time it takes to get a car loaded with a self loaderchanged light duty towing for the better," says Sawyers."It became a much safer industry." "Crazy Dave" Craze later formed Recovery Solutions in Chesapeake, Va., to manufacture his invention and additional products based on his design. Recovery Solutions offers four series of wheel lifts and a large selection of parts and accessories as well.

In 2002, towing veteran Carnell Duvall, owner of Duvall Wrecker Service in Quinton, Okla., patented a new device, the Rollback Sidewinder. A vehicle-positioning system, the Rollback Sidewinder arranges wrecked vehicles on the shoulder in exact loading position without crossing the centerline. "The machine is wireless remote-controlled and can be operated up to 200 feet away, which is a big safety plus," says Duvall. "The highway patrol always appreciates you working wrecks without crossing the center line."

Duvall also introduced the Off-Road Recovery Skid Steer Device. The device mounts on skid steer loaders by quick attach and is used when four-wheel drive wreckers cannot get to the scene because of surface road conditions caused by rain, snow or ice. "The skid steer device has tool boxes for chains, a stabilizing system, and a choice of three winches—9,000, 12,000 or 15,000 pounds—equipped with 100 feet of cable," explains Duvall.

End of the line

As new, high-tech products come to market, some traditional tools of the trade have been retired to the boneyard. The wheel lift, for example, replaced the sling as the gear of choice for towing vehicles. "The sling has become a secondary device as opposed to the primary device for light-duty towing," says Sawyers. "There are still some sling trucks out there, but the wheel lift—self-loading or conventional—really dominates the light-duty part of the industry now."

Strickland's shop takes a different approach: "We've mostly eliminated our conventional sling-type and wheel-lift wreckers and replaced them with carriers," he says."If a damagedvehicle needs a tow from a recovery scene, it is very possible that hook-up with a wheel lift may not be possible and further damage may result froma sling hook-up. This makes the rollback the tool of choice for us."

Over at Dakota Towing, Al Gregg fondly recalls using pan dollies during recovery operations. Once a standard tool for light-duty towing, Gregg's pan dollies are no longer in active use—"although," he says, "I still have a set in the shed."

Bob's Garage & Towing, Inc., recently transitioned its light and medium-duty truck fleet to newer models. "We have used Vulcan wheel-lift wreckers since the late 1980s when they were first introduced on the market," says Jared Fox. Bob's original light and medium-duty fleet included a 1997 International 4700 with Chevron 19-foot flatbed, a 1999 International 4700 with Vulcan 894 wheel lift system, a 2000 Ford F450 with a Vulcan 881 wheel lift, and a 2001 International 4700 with a Chevron 21-foot flatbed.

Bob's recently updated its fleet, purchasing a 2007 Ford F550 with a Jerr-Dan HPL-3500 single-line wrecker, a 2006 Ford F650 with a Vulcan 894 twin-line wrecker, and a 2006 Ford F650 with a Chevron 21-foot flatbed Series 14. Also in the fleet are a 2000 Chevrolet 3500 with a Vulcan 807R autogrip with extendable boom and single line, and a 2001 Chevrolet 3500 with a 19-foot Champion flatbed.

When Bob's Garage & Towing expanded into the heavy-duty towing and recovery arena, a completely refurbished, low-mileage 1996 Chevy Kodiak with a Century 4024 wrecker was the first addition. Next, in January 2004, they added a 1997 Freightliner FLD120 with an Aatac Titan 50 wrecker. The Freightliner was replaced in May 2007 by a 2004 Peterbilt 378 with a Century 9055 wrecker which is also equipped with dual SP850 side-pullers. To keep its lineup fresh, the company is planning to add a new wrecker, a flatbed and a road tractor in the near future.

Don't go lightly

Knowledge is crucial, says Charles Rash, who urges towers to participate in their national, state, and local towing associations. "If you are not involved," he says, "then you're just on the sidelines watching, and you are going backwards in your business."

Rash says that his family business has been involved in local politics since the company launched in the 1930s, and have been involved in lawmaking as well. "For 75 years our family has put in our two cents' worth, for and against towing regulations," he explains. "Texas politics are tough, but I've found that the returns have been immeasurable." In fact, he says, "I've found that people who don't like their regulations didn't get involved in the writing of them."

Rash urges tow company owners to focus on the important things. "I can't understand an owner who spends thousands of dollars on a fancy paint job and then sits in a meeting and cries about the cost of training and association dues," he laments. "Maybe they need to cut the rig off their truck and sell watermelons on the side of the road instead." In a business where light-duty towing is getting more attention, the prepared tower stands to benefit the most.

Light-Duty Recovery: A Conversation with Jason Strickland

Jason Strickland is the owner of Strickland Towing in Haven, Kan., which has offered light-, medium- and heavy-duty towing services since 1998. Strickland Towing primarily uses rollbacks for towing rather than sling or wheel-lift wreckers.

Most of our light duty rollover recoveries are performed with rollbacks. First, at any accident scene we perform a safety and site assessment, looking for factors such as lane blockage, fuel spills, battery location/condition, if vehicle is in or out of gear, ignition turned off, and any physical obstructions that will make the recovery more difficult.

If the vehicle is on its top, we attach chains around the frame (avoiding, wires, lines, etc.). If the frame is not exposed, we hook to the reinforced frame slots using a bridle. We slowly and cautiously winch the vehicle back onto the side that has already been damaged first. Once the vehicle is resting on its side, we gently pull the vehicle back onto its wheels and prepare it for tow.

If the vehicle is on its side parallel to the highway and facing away from our recovery unit, many times we use the reverse roll method. We attach a strap to the frame down low on the side facing away from our unit. If necessary, we dig a tunnel between the ground and the side of the vehicle resting on the ground and run the strap through it back to our winch line. As we winch the strap to the unit, the vehicle then rolls back onto its wheels.

In some instances with the above-mentioned scenario, we have had the luck to have a sturdy tree in the area and used the tree as a dead man to perform a rollover. This method is performed by running the cable from our unit to a snatch block chained around the tree, and then attaching the cable to the vehicles. This isn't common occurrence, but once in a while luck is on our side.

If steering components are damaged or missing, we use an 8' long oak 4"x4" as a skate to center the car on the deck. We also use floor jacks, snatch blocks and other cribbage to maneuver the cars on the decks. In most cases, we do not use a rollover stick, but sometimes they are a necessity.

Propane Truck Recoveries

Propane — just one of the many hazardous materials that towers face when called to recover a disabled vehicle. Because of its flammability, propane can be one of the riskiest liquids on the road. A rollover, impact or other damage to a propane tank can trigger catastrophic results, from a small spill to a gigantic fireball.

Because of the product's volatility, it's even more important to consider all risk factors before proceeding with the recovery of a propane truck. "Towers should understand the hazards associated with the incident and the importance of conducting a hazard assessment before moving it," says Stuart Flatow, vice president of safety and training at the Propane Education & Research Council in Washington, D.C.

Also critical, adds Flatow, is for towers to understand their role in the decision-making process when a propane-carrying vehicle needs to be offloaded. "There are stability concerns, proper rigging issues and limitations of the lifting lugs on a cargo tank," he explains.

Recovering propane

Once at the scene, towers have a lengthy checklist of items to consider, says Curt Sharp of Merl's Towing Service in Grand Rapids, Mich. "These considerations include the type of product that you are working with, the stability of the product, type of containers it will be transported in, weather conditions, environmental issues, public safety and concern, and of course the area in which the accident occurred."

In some ways, one HAZMAT can be quite similar to another. Jared Fox of Bob's Garage & Towing, Inc., in Painesville, Ohio, notes that the response to a propane incident isn't much different than the response for other incidents involving liquid flammables. "This type of load is going to be under considerable pressure," he says. "But it's most stable when it remains condensed and under pressure — vice a product that has been, for example, unloaded from the tanker."

The biggest risk of injury and damage when working with casualties containing propane is a BLEVE, or boiling liquid expanding vapor explosion. A BLEVE occurs when the pressure in the tank exceeds that at which the safety relief valve can properly vent the excess pressure into the outside atmosphere. Typically this pressure increase is caused by fire impinging on the tank. "A BLEVE is going to incinerate anything in the immediate area and send the container airborne," warns Fox.

Offloading

In certain situations, offloading the propane might be a preferred option. According to Sharp, depending on the location, condition, and position of the vessel that's transporting the propane, offloading might not be possible. In some cases, he says, the load might need to be "burned off" in a controlled burn. Either option is typically handled by a HAZMAT team or, in certain cases, the company that's transporting the propane.

If propane is unloaded, says Fox, the tank needs to be flushed with an inert gas like nitrogen. "Otherwise you will be left with a tank that is still filled with a highly explosive vapor cloud," he explains. If a fire does occur, says Fox, "Only once the fire department has extinguished the fire and removed the life-safety hazards would any recovery actions begin."

When working with local government agencies, be prepared for different levels of capability, says Sharp. "Most local fire departments or first responders are not trained, equipped, or otherwise able to offload and handle such cargo," he notes. In these cases, the tower's expertise is critical.

In Sierra Vista, Ariz., Barnett's Towing LLC has the unique situation of owning a retail propane distributor, Barnett's Propane. "We have bobtail delivery trucks for residential delivery," says Troy Barnett, vice president of the company. "Barnett's Propane Transport is the bulk transportation division. This division uses seven tractor-trailer transport units to haul propane from the distribution points to other retailers." All told, the company's towing fleet consists of 58 tow truck and support vehicles, while the propane fleet has 26 vehicles.

Because of Barnett's unique setup, the towing division is quite knowledgeable about propane truck recoveries. "In the history of Barnett's we have recovered over 20 propane vehicle accidents," says Barnett. "Our knowledge of the product is a large reason we are called to the incidents in this state." The towing division, in business since 1963, has four locations in the state and handles light- to heavy-duty recoveries.

To get up to speed on propane recoveries, Barnett recommends that towers consult with companies in their area. "Towers often work and train with fire and police departments," he says. "I feel that towers need to go out and meet with propane companies *before* the wreck happens. This would solve a lot of on-scene mistakes and could prevent someone from getting hurt — or worse."

Local government and law enforcement agencies

This rule of thumb applies to other organizations as well. Flatow echoes Barnett's recommendation: "I suggest that towers reach out and get to know local enforcement and propane marketers prior to any response," says Flatow. "This ensures that they have the correct equipment to conduct the job. More often than not, a 'regular' tow truck will not cut it," he says.

"Typically in a situation of a propane vessel being involved in an accident, local government agencies will work to control the spread of a fire," says Sharp. In addition, he says, they might spray a tank to cool it off and perform traffic and crowd control duties including evacuations.

"Police are responsible for maintaining scene security, accident investigation and traffic flow or road closure depending on the situation," says Fox. "In many cases where a casualty is a propane tanker, evacuation and road closure are going to be necessary to ensure civilian safety." Meanwhile, the fire department will handle human casualties, fire suppression and prevention, and supervision of recovery efforts.

Safety issues

According to Sharp, propane is typically transported in very strong high-pressure tanks that usually remain intact during an accident. For towers, he says, "the most common concerns are vapor expansion within the tank which can be caused by the ambient temperature at the scene rising, either due to a fire or local weather conditions. At times it may be difficult for the tank to vent itself after an accident due to the position it rests in and the location of the safety vents on the tank." In worst-case scenarios this situation can result in a BLEVE.

Sometimes the tank can be punctured during recovery operations. If this happens, says Fox, "all operations come to a stop until the contents can be controlled or moved to prevent fire or, worse, an explosion." This is the biggest hazard for this type of cargo, he adds. "Sudden fire on a puncture or leak can quickly cause the contents to explode." For this reason, Fox reiterates the need for fire department personnel to be present in order to ensure that procedures are done properly.

For background reading, Flatow recommends the book *Propane Emergencies, 3rd Edition*, which can be purchased at www.propanecatalog.com or downloaded from his organization's Web site at www.propanesafety.com. The book has a companion guide for training facilitators.

Flatow also lists as additional resources the various state gas associations and propane marketers, as well as local, state and national towing associations.

Training needed

"Lack of proper training can result in a catastrophic ending and could seriously injure or kill someone," says Fox. Sharp notes that the towing and recovery industry offers limited training in handling these kinds of HAZMAT accidents. "The training that you can receive usually comes from other HAZMAT companies or training organizations, or the transportation companies that are involved with these loads," he says.

Real-world training can make all the difference. "Our recovery operators attend in-class and hands-onseminars," says Fox. "I'm working closely with Steve Dressler — a 20-year veteran of the towing industry and senior driver at Bob's Garage and Towing, Inc. — to develop further training opportunities with our local fire department." The goal: to make the responders' jobs easier to do and to create a safe working environment when pulling crippled propane trucks off the road.

In-house training at the company has consisted of not only heavy recovery but also HAZMAT certification via the local fire chief. In addition, drivers receive online training in NIMS, the National Incident Management System developed and deployed by the Federal Emergency Management Agency. Sharp also points to the Internet as a valuable training resource. As part of their training program, he and his drivers accumulate as much information as they can from the Web.

Recently Fox's company participated in an exclusive three-day training program held at a local chemical facility. The towers' classmates included local fire departments and rescue, recovery and HAZMAT personnel along with officials from the county government. The purpose of the training program was for the various organizations to learn and practice each group's role in a tanker emergency. By doing so, the public safety agencies were able to get a glimpse of the capabilities and skills that the towing company could provide during this type of emergency.

On the final day the class was challenged with several full-size scenarios on which to practice what they'd learned. To maintain a sense of urgency, "We had no idea what the scenarios would be," says Fox. "This was just like the real thing: radio communications, each team was sent in as the order it would follow — the fire department, police department, HAZMAT and the towing company. And no one knew what the incident was until they arrived on scene."

In one scenario a tanker loaded with diesel fuel rolled over on its side. (Water was used to simulate the diesel.) HAZMAT specialists pumped all but a couple thousand gallons of fuel out of the tank. Then the towers were given the go-ahead to upright the truck. Recovery operators Steve Dressler, Jared Fox and Randy Sullivan along with company president Jay Fox participated in the scenario. "We used our Century 4024 20-ton wrecker to lift the nose of the tanker and place one six-by-six timber to get the nose off the ground for our endless recovery straps," says Fox. His company also provided a fully equipped incident response trailer.

Next, Fox and his team positioned their Century 9055 50-ton with XP850 side pullers to the belly side of the tanker. "To get the initial lift, we attached the two lines off the rear to two endless loops applied over the top at the front and rear of the tanker," recalls Fox. To create a controlled roll, Fox then rigged XP850 winches off snatch blocks from the top of the boom to the side of the tanker belly.

("Bear in mind," says Fox, "in an actual emergency when faced with a fully loaded tanker, at least four straps should be used to equally distribute the weight of the tank along the trailer frame to maintain the integrity of the casualty.")

"Please take as much training as possible," urges Fox. "There is always something to learn, and it's well worth any price to gain advancement in your career and do the job right so everyone goes home safe!"

Local or over-the-road?

Towers recover more local fuel delivery trucks than long-haul transporters. It's the law of averages, since local trucks make frequent deliveries to residential and commercial locations, increasing the chances of an accident. "The local delivery trucks seem to get themselves into stickier situations when they're delivering to a home," says Fox. "The work area can be confined, and low-hanging wires can be encountered — not to mention the possibility of unusual grade changes. In the event of a problem, the life-safety hazard is much higher due to the more densely populated area of a local neighborhood."

Regarding the recovery itself, "both types of units are basically the same to handle," explains Sharp. "Just the volume of propane is different." Often the bigger and louder transport vessel receives more press. "The over-the-road tankers seem to make for a more 'dramatic' and newsworthy accident scene, which is unfortunate because any size vessel — including rail cars — can cause dramatic effects," says Sharp.

Tricky propane recoveries can test the tower's training and inventiveness. For best results, be alert and prepared, says Sharp. "It is very important to understand what your capabilities are and where your limits are set," he says. "Knowing when to ask for help or when to walk away from a job are just as important as knowing how to do a job!"

"As with almost any recovery," says Sharp, "no two HAZMAT recoveries are the same."

Anatomy of a Propane Truck Recovery

On the morning of August 8, 2007, Merl›s Towing Service of Grand Rapids, Mich., responded to a tractor/trailer loaded with propane that had rolled over approximately 60 miles from the towing company. "We were given minimal information at first, except that the unit had left the roadway, crossed the ditch, and rolled over," recalls Curt Sharp. He drove to the accident scene in a Kenworth/Century 60 ton rotator, followed by Adam Schmidt in a Kenworth/Century 9055. They were joined by Mark Fredette with a Freightliner/Century 3212 and the company's air-cushion recovery trailer.

It was a hot, humid day with clear skies and temperatures hovering around 90 degrees. Upon arriving at the accident site, Sharp and Schmidt spoke with the Michigan State Police motor carrier officer, Michigan Department of Transportation officials, and local fire department personnel.

Also on scene was another towing company that had originally been called to help. Unfortunately those towers were not equipped to handle a tanker rollover. "They asked that we invoice them for their time on scene and they left," says Sharp. The team from Merl's Towing Service then began an on-scene survey.

The casualty was a 2004 Freightliner Columbia with an 11,200-gallon

MC331 tank loaded with propane.Sharp and his team estimated the total weight at 80,000 pounds. Recalls Sharp: "The unit left the right side of the roadway, traveled approximately 450 feet, took out a fence and several small trees, then climbed the side of a steep hill before rolling over on the driver's side."It came to rest 120 feet from the highway shoulder.

Between the tanker and the tree-lined highway stood a fence and a swampy ditch of 30 to 40 feet in width. "The hill above the tractor and tanker was a berm that bordered a golf course," says Sharp. Golf course management refused to allow the towers access from their side of the accident. "The challenge was getting recovery equipment close enough to the casualty," he adds.

Fortunately the temperature and pressure of the propane were found to be stable. A minor amount of motor oil had leaked from the truck's damaged oil cooler. In addition, a small amount of hydraulic fluid was leaking from a vented cap, which was quickly sealed. The motor carrier officer monitored and logged the status every 30 minutes.

To give Sharp's team enough room to maneuver safely, DOT closed down all but one lane to traffic, providing the towers one lane and the shoulder to stage their equipment. With this done, it was time to create a recovery plan. The towers again met with the Motor Carrier Officer, MDOT, the fire department, and (by telephone) the manager of the transport company.

"The team discussed many options," says Sharp, "including lifting the casualty with large cranes, excavating part of the berm, or building a road to get trucks into the scene.With the casualty lying on a golf course, protecting the property and environment were both concerns." Using a crane was eliminated as an option due to travel, setup and excavation requirements. Since the golf course wouldn't allow anyone to dig up the berm, the towers were left with one option: build their own access path.

Should the propane load be moved or offloaded? The motor carrier officer would make that decision, but only after the tanker was uprighted. A local excavating company bulldozed away several damaged trees and leveled an access path. Meanwhile the propane transport company brought a tractor and empty propane tank in case they were needed.

Uprighting the fallen tanker was a tricky procedure. "We knew that the initial lift was going to be the most difficult because of how the casualty was positioned and the limited amount of room to perform a top lift," says Sharp. He and his team were familiar with Hulcher Services, a railroad contracting firm with a terminal just 100 miles away in Hammond, Ind. Hulcher responded within two hours, providing specialty equipment and a rigging/safety crew.

"The front of the casualty tractor was repositioned with the excavator's dozer," recalls Sharp. "We rigged the casualty tractor to be pulled down with that same dozer, operated by the crew from Hulcher Services. We decided to rig the front of the propane tank for a top lift using one of the side boom tractors. The rear of the tanker was rigged to winch from the bottom, around the tank (using a 24-inch nylon strap) with the second tractor."

"We positioned the tractor with a side boom at the front of the trailer on the topside to finish pre-lift rigging," says Sharp. The front of the tanker was rigged to support the initial lift, which was estimated at 20,000 pounds. To help with pullover, the other tractor was placed at the top of the berm, inline with the rear axles of the tanker. "Rigging for this end was attached to the front trailer axle with a screw pin shackle attached to a 24-inch nylon strap going under and around the top of the tank," explains Sharp. Then the 100,000-pound rear winch of the Hulcher Services tractor was hooked to this strap.

With the equipment in place, the recovery team completed a walkaround. "We did not feel the need for a control vehicle since the unit would have to be winched all the way down and held on the side of the hill," says Sharp.

The State Police shut down the remainder of the highway and recovery operations began. "The casualty stood up with relative ease and was held (on the low side) by the side boom tractor," says Sharp. "The rear rigging was broken down, and that tractor was repositioned behind the casualty to winch the unit out to the road. The low side tractor remained hooked to the front of the trailer and walked out beside the trailer as it was being winched out."

With the crippled tanker now accessible, the towers removed their rigging so the motor carrier officer could inspect the tank. Fortunately the tank had sustained no structural damage and could be transported without offloading the propane. The damaged tractor was removed and

113

replaced with a working one, and the transport company drove the tanker back to their facility.

After some grading and cleanup, Young's Environmental Company of Grand Rapids removed the small amounts of leaked fluid. Their job done, the men from Merl's Towing returned to their shop. Total time from port to port, including equipment cleanup, was 11 hours.

Auto Hauling and Tarps

Need your vehicle moved from one state to another? Perhaps it's more than just a car to you — it's your "baby," and it needs extra care while being transported. For some car owners, a vehicle is an expensive investment — a prized Corvette or European sports car, for example. Or maybe it's a secret prototype designed in an automaker's engineering laboratory, ready for unveiling at an upcoming auto show.

Whatever the vehicle, it needs to be protected from the elements. Water spots, chips from flying asphalt, bird droppings — any one of these can crush the value of an automobile, expensive or not. Fortunately, rollbacks equipped with quality tarpaulins, along with trucks and trailers built specifically to haul automobiles, stand ready to help at a variety of companies across the United States.

Towers who haul

Some of these companies exist solely to move vehicles across the country and all around the world. Some are brokers, working the telephones to finagle transport for their customers through contract transporters. And then there are the towing firms that include auto hauling in their menu of services.

Jesse DeGraeve, owner of Anytime Towing in Traverse City, Mich., is a former automotive engineer. Four years ago he was looking for a change of career, so he took a hard look at the towing industry. "I noticed that there was a lack of customer service at existing towing companies in town," he says. "I figured that if I started a company that concentrated on customer service, it would not be very hard to break into the business." DeGraeve got a Freightliner flatbed and opened his business in a local industrial park, offering light- and medium-duty towing services.

Business grew steadily. Today DeGraeve's shop has six trucks: two Freightliner FL60 Flatbeds, a Kenworth T300 flatbed, a Dodge 5500 wrecker, a Ford F-350 wrecker and a Freightliner tractor with afour-car wedge trailer for hauling cars.*American Towman* magazine honored DeGraeve's shop with its customer service excellence award for three years in a row.

Anytime Towing offers auto transport anywhere in the United States. "We've hauled a little bit of everything," says DeGraeve, "from tractors and construction equipment to Porsches, classic cars and everything in between." Although it's common practice to subcontract the hauling to other companies, DeGraeve keeps the entire operation under his own roof. "As far as not subcontracting goes," he explains, "we stay away from that because I would rather not have another company doing work under our name. If there is damage to a vehicle, the customer is looking to us, not who we hired to do the job. It is just a lot simpler to do the work ourselves," he says. "Then we can do a better job of quality control and customer service."

Meanwhile, at Schmit Towing, owners Steve and Sue Schmit own five flatbeds and two triple-car trailers for long-distance hauling. The Minneapolis, Minn.-based company is family owned and operated and is currently celebrating its 25th anniversary. How did the Schmits get into the auto hauling business? "It came along with the territory," says Steve Schmit. "Over the years as we added dealerships as regular customers, they would also have us move their cars around the area."

During the regular workday, Schmit notes that his drivers pick up every type of vehicle at accident scenes and from clients who want their vehicles transported to dealers or repair shops. "We'll haul Hondas, SUVs, all the way to brand-new vehicles bought and sold on eBay, and collector and specialty cars," says Schmit. The most interesting vehicles he deals with are the eBay purchases, which include hot rods and muscle cars. It can be tough to haul an amazing car and not be able to test-drive it, says Schmit. "You'd just love to take them for a ride, but you can't do it," he chuckles.

Schmit's trailer and flatbeds see a lot of use in transporting and delivering vehicles all around the Midwest. "We have one client who does a lot of car shipping all over the world," says Schmit. "The client brings cars to us — usually eight or 10 cars off an auto transport carrier. Then we'll deliver those cars to the customers in the Midwest." The opposite is also true: Schmit's company picks up cars around the Midwest and brings them back to the company's terminal. After that, a transport truck takes the cars and delivers them to the customers.

Haulers who move

There are also companies that deal strictly with transport and have branched out to include auto hauling. Kings Park, N.Y., is home to Plycon Transportation Group, a nationwide logistics specialist. Founded by the late Arthur Pliaconis in 1982, the company is now run by his three sons, David, Dean and Chris. Plycon has grown to include over 200 trucks and 11 locations coast to coast. "Our expertise is in handling items of great value, from fine furniture manufacturers to interior designers, architects, white glove in-home service or individual pieces of furniture and now your fine automobile," says Chris Pliaconis, vice president of Plycon.

At Plycar, the fine automotive transportation division of the company, "We realize character is everything," explains Plyconis, "from selecting all our drivers foremost for their professionalism and their interpersonal skills, to our commitment of providing you with the highest level of quality service in the industry."

Preparation of the automobile is critical to ensure its safe delivery, no matter where the final destination is.Plycar, for example, asks clients to leave at least one-eighth and at most a quarter tank of gas in the vehicle, and to disconnect any racks and covers that could come off or be damaged during transport. The standard warning about removing personal items from the vehicle applies here as well. The carrier's insurance plan doesn't cover your favorite sunglasses, iPod or winter coat.

Another option for customers who want to transport vehicles is to engage a middleman to make the arrangements. "We are an auto transportation brokerage instead of a true carrier," explains Randy Bond of ATS Transportation Services in Gilroy, Calif. Bond founded ATS in 1989 after earning his stripes at a major steamship agency and at an international freight forwarder. At ATS, "we interface with truckers, tow companies, and customers," he explains. ATS moves vehicles using car carriers, flatbeds, enclosed carriers, ocean carriers and even aircraft.

Fancy cars

Over-the-road transport sometimes calls for very specific equipment. Schmit towing has an enclosed trailer that the company uses to transport specialty vehicles — expensive foreign sports cars, for example. Recently that trailer came in handy when a brand-new exotic sports car was unloaded from a train. The dealer's representative got in and turned the key, but the car wouldn't start.

Schmit's phone rang almost immediately afterward. It was the auto dealership, which cut a deal for Schmit to pick the car up and deliver it to the dealer's shop for repairs. The key to the agreement was that Schmit would use his special enclosed trailer: "The manufacturer of the car didn't want the public to see their fancy automobile on the back of a flatbed," he explains.

Sometimes the transporters are asked to move cars to auto shows or exhibitions. "We haul cars from the new car dealers to the big auto show here in Minneapolis every year," says Schmit. The job is routine, he says: put brand-new vehicles on the back of a flatbed truck, drop them off in the morning, and pick them up in the evening. Once the vehicle is unloaded at the exhibition site, other people take over. "Usually we'll drive into the building and unload the car. A lot of these buildings have big doors where trucks can pull in so they're out of the weather."

To familiarize his staff with auto transport, Schmit does in-house training, showing new drivers how to haul vehicles safely and damage-free. "It's not complicated," he says. "It just takes a little caution." After learning the ropes, he adds, the drivers catch on quickly. Local regulations are important as well. "There are rules on how the car is fastened," notes DeGraeve. "In Michigan it is a law to have to lights on a vehicle you are towing." For commercial vehicles like DeGraeve's trucks, the same rules apply, he says — "otherwise you might have to answer to the Department of Transportation."

Technological advancements are making the job safer behind the wheel and on the road. "The equipment out there seems to be getting better and better," says DeGraeve. "We have stainless steel wrecker beds, wireless tow lights, LED lighting, computers — all these little things add up at the end of the day."

In Calabasas, Calif., Jeff Littman of Century Towing cautions his fellow towers about insurance requirements for hauling expensive vehicles, pointing out a common misconception in the industry: "If your policy says you have $1 million in coverage, that's $1 million if you crash into a building. Your 'on the hook' coverage is the hard part," he explains.

For transporting expensive vehicles, the typical towers' insurance probably won't do, says Littman. "The average guy hauling vehicles might have a $75,000 insurance policy, which isn't enough. This is what separates the men from the boys." Littman explains that a policy that would cover an expensive vehicle — something in the neighborhood of $500,000 worth of coverage — can cost an additional $1,500 to $1,800 per month. That's a high price to pay for towers who want to haul expensive vehicles from point to point — but it can be well worth the expense in a business that revolves around getting from Point A to Point B as safely as possible.

Covering Cars with Superman's Cape:
Rolling Tarp Systems for Auto Hauling

Towers using rollback trucks for hauling automobiles have been rewarded with a new product: the sliding tarp system, with models available from

Jerr-Dan and Miller Industries. One operator can roll the tarp right over the vehicle he's carrying, protecting it from the elements — and from prying eyes, whether it's an expensive sports car or a hush-hush prototype. "The guy hauling a Lamborghini or Ferrari probably doesn't want people to know he has that kind of car going down the road," says Alan Briley, Director of Sales for Indianapolis-based Aero Industries, which has built tarps for flatbeds and trailers for nearly 65 years. "So the only way to take care of it is to climb up there and cover it."

The sliding tarp system provides an alternate, and safer, method for the tower. "The biggest benefit from a sliding tarp system is that it keeps the driver on the ground," says Briley. "He's not climbing up on the body of the truck to cover the vehicle." For anyone who's dealt with worker's compensation issues resulting from driver injuries, the rolling tarp provides some relief: "Keeping the driver's feet on the ground is worth a lot more than the price of the system," notes Briley. An additional benefit: add graphics and text and the tarp can function as a "rolling billboard" — a useful marketing tool for advertising a company's services.

Jerr-Dan teamed up with Aero Industries, which has manufactured the popular Conestoga sliding tarp system since the early 1980s. "Jerr-Dan came to us after doing extensive market research," explains Briley. "They determined that there was a market for sliding tarp systems, specifically in the carrier industry." The target markets included luxury high-end vehicles, auctions, and industrial carriers of equipment like backhoes, bulldozers and the like.

Meanwhile, Miller Industries got together with Quick Draw Tarpaulin Systems of Dearborn, Mich., to offer their own jointly produced system. "We met with Miller at a towing show," recalls Jim Payne of Quick Draw Tarps. "The conversation started there. We decided we should look into doing something together, and to see if it was a win-win for both companies." The result was a Quick Draw Tarp that can be installed on rollback trucks.

Another use for the rolling tarp system is to cover vehicles that are being held as evidence for forensic study. "For a crime scene investigation," says Payne, "if it's a fatality and they can't put anything over the vehicle, it can be put right up on a truck. Then the tarp can be rolled right over the vehicle so that nothing touches it."

Jeff Littman, owner of Century Towing in Calabasas, Calif., uses an enclosed trailer to transport his customers' high-end vehicles. While he's examined the new tarps on the market, for now it's not cost-effective for him to make the jump.

"The tarps cost around $15,000 each and are restricted to one truck," explains Littman. "On the other hand, my enclosed trailer cost about $12,000 and it's pretty versatile." In particular, he notes that certain tarps must be installed at the manufacturer's factory, which could be on the opposite side of the country. "So if you have a truck in southern California and you want to have a tarp installed, you're going to have to drive it 6,000 miles and then pay $15,000 for the tarp," he says.

Still, even a cross-country trip to have the right tarp installed can be worth the effort. A high-quality protective cover that doubles as a rolling billboard can be a useful addition to an existing equipment fleet — and an opportunity to expand the various services that a towing company offers to its customers.

Advanced Tanker Recovery

What are the best methods for rescuing crippled tanker trucks? Wes
Wilburn and Tom Luciano sponsor hands-on courses to provide the
answers. Both men are highly regarded training instructors, and their
classes have been a consistent draw for towers across North America and
elsewhere.

Wilburn runs Tow Co-Op, a membership-based club that provides
products and services via cooperative buying efforts. Luciano is the
northeast regional sales manager for Vulcan and Miller Industries.
"Tanker recovery is one of Tom's passions," says Wilburn. "His strong
mechanical background and vast experience make him a natural to lead
the instruction for this highly specialized class."

Just like real life

For the best hands-on training, Wilburn swears by lifelike field exercises using real equipment. "Over the years I have learned that most mistakes that happen on a complex heavy-duty recovery can be traced back to the original decisions of what equipment to use and where things are placed," he explains. "By showing the students what to do in a simulated environment, they'll be better prepared to deal with the real thing." From positioning equipment effectively to figuring out where to hook onto the tanker, Wilburn stresses careful planning at all times.

Before performing surgery on a tanker incident, Wilburn believes that the tower needs to understand the patient. During their courses, for example, Wilburn and Luciano first cover the details of how a tanker is constructed. That technical information comes in handy in the field, when towers might be faced with unusual incident scenes that require more than simply pulling a tanker into an upright position.

Faced with multiple options, how can a tower decide the best way to rescue a downed tanker? There are advantages to working the job from the top side instead of the bottom side of the tank, says Wilburn, who recommends using a digital strain gauge to track how the force is being applied. The tool helps the tower make more efficient use of his or her time at the accident site, providing accurate numbers and eliminating guesswork. By utilizing the strongest points of the tank, towers can make the most complicated recoveries seem easy. "With the cost of new equipment, does it make any sense not to work your equipment easier?" says Wilburn.

Proper placement

When working the top side of a tanker, Wilburn points to several key actions that will make for a successful recovery. First, take the time to install properly sized and rated snatch blocks in each line prior to making the lift.

Also take a close look at the placement of the truck and the boom, says Wilburn. The operator has placed outriggers to give the rotator its best possible stance. In addition, the boom is placed out and over the load so that the operator could work the winches rather than the boom. "This is important for many reasons," explains Wilburn, "including creating a safer working environment for everyone by raising the load with the winch."

This technique can keep accidents from occurring during the recovery process. If a tower booms up with a load and the equipment suddenly experiences a hydraulic failure of some sort — a hydraulic line blowing out, for example — most booms will fall as the safety valve closes shut. "As the valve slams shut, this will catch the falling boom," says Wilburn, "but it will also shock load the entire system."

Could the unit in our example have been lifted without using snatch blocks? "Probably, maybe," says Wilburn. But, he says, since the cable was the weakest point in this particular lift, using snatch blocks reduced the load on the cable, winches and entire boom structure.

Air cushions

Air cushions are another tool that Wilburn and Luciano like to use when recovering tankers. During the classes they teach, "We perform a complete recovery using the cushions in conjunction with heavy duty wreckers," says Wilburn. "Using air cushions is an art form unto itself." Add a loaded tanker that needs to be uprighted, and the tower has quite a challenge to solve.

Wilburn notes that air cushions are placed starting at the rear and working forward. And once the job is done, towers should take extra care with their air cushions. "Having the air cushions stored away properly after the last job really dictates how the next job will go," says Wilburn. "I am not only talking about having them cleaned up, which should be obvious to most. What I believe is critical is how they have the air removed and how they are 'tucked,' so to speak." Wilburn recommends that towers tuck three sides of each cushion and let the side with the hose stay untucked. "From my experience, this works much better," he says.

But what if the tower doesn't have air cushions available during a recovery? Not a problem, says Wilburn: during their classes, he and Luciano host several "wrecker only" field scenarios involving heavy-duty trucks and recovery straps only.

Wilburn looks forward to teaching another advanced tanker recovery course this year. The host company, John's Towing & Recovery of Durham, N.C., is well equipped for hands-on instruction in tanker recovery techniques. "They own tractors, tankers, and many other items," he explains. "They obtained them over the years strictly for the purpose of doing high-level training."

Military Recovery Specialists

It was April 2004, and the First Battle of Fallujah was underway. Near the Iraqi city a U.S. Army observation helicopter had been shot down and lay crippled on the ground. A cordon of military vehicles encircled the crash site, protecting the disabled chopper. Army Sgt. 1st Class Sean Dewitt rolled his M88 recovery vehicle into the area. All around him, enemy small arms fire chattered in the pitch-black night.

It was the most difficult recovery job of his career. "The helicopter had been shot down right outside of the city," recalls Dewitt. The 82nd Airborne Division had secured the accident scene. "I've never seen so many armored vehicles protecting one site," remembers Dewitt. "We went out there and hooked up the helicopter safely." An 18-wheeler flatbed truck was right behind Dewitt. "We picked up the helicopter, had the flatbed back up underneath it, lowered the helicopter and then strapped it down real good." Then, job done, "we got it out of there."

Though they operate behind the scenes and with little fanfare,

127

ALLAN T. DUFFIN

military recovery specialists are critical to the units with which they serve, whether at home or deployed to hot spots like the current battlefields in Iraq and Afghanistan. Combat scenarios like the one described by Sean Dewitt happen periodically in Iraq, where even recovery vehicles have been turned into weapons: During one incident, a suicide bomber packed a tow truck with explosives, drove into a bustling commercial area in the city of Hillah, south of Baghdad, and detonated his payload. Two dozen Iraqis died and 69 were wounded in the ensuing fireball.

Although different branches of the military — Army, Navy, Marine Corps, and Air Force — all have some type of "motor pool" for their vehicles, they don't all use the same type of tow truck. At Marine Corps Base Camp Pendleton, a sprawling facility of more than 125,000 acres in Southern California, one of the vehicles that Sergeant Robert Short operates is the MK36, a 6-by-6 wrecker built by Oshkosh Truck. The MK36 is a variant of the Medium Tactical Replacement Vehicle, or MTVR, which is used by the Navy and Marine Corps for a number of all-terrain purposes including cargo hauling and resupply. "It's outfitted with a winch and a lifting cylinder," says Short, "plus a crane as well as a lifting arm."

Like the civilian towing industry, the military routinely refreshes its fleet of towing equipment as new technology and new requirements pop up. When the Marines upgrade their heavy equipment, they naturally needed a larger tow vehicle for recovery operations. When Marines stationed in Okinawa received the MK36 two years ago, they appreciated the improved capability of the new wrecker.

"Almost every motor transport unit has gotten rid of their five-ton vehicles, which is the most weight the old wreckers were capable of lifting," Gunnery Sgt. Benjamin Douglas, a recovery vehicle operator, told the *Okinawa Marine* newspaper at the time. Due to its ability to lift seven tons instead of just five, Douglas added, "[The MK36] will drastically cut down the man hours and work time it takes to recover a vehicle."

Back at Camp Pendleton, Sergeant Short, originally from Bridgeville, Del., has experience across a wide spectrum of Marine Corps vehicles. "I've done everything from motor recovery to civilian recovery and heavy

128

equipment recovery," he says. Much of his work has been done in Iraq, where he has served three tours of duty.

Short adds that he has worked alongside civilian recovery specialists during his time overseas. "If a civilian vehicle was disabled," he says, "civilian towers were dispatched to go out with us to pick it up." According to Short, the assistance of civilian towing contractors was a big help in a combat zone where the workload was already hectic: "It's one less thing we had to worry about." Also, notes Short, "We compared notes and learn from each other."

Not all of Short's memories of his time in Iraq center around combat situations. On a humorous note, he recalls the day that he was tasked to pull several disabled Humvees out of a ditch full of wastewater. "That was no fun," he laughs. "As I was working, the ground gave way and I fell in underneath the wastewater." One recovery and one shower later, Short was back at work.

So why do soldiers join the motor pool? "I've always been a mechanic," says Sgt. 1st Class Robert Slusher, a native of Wallace, Idaho, who is assigned to Bravo Company, 101st Forward Support Battalion, 1st Brigade, 1st Infantry Division, our of Fort Riley, Kan. "I started working on cars in high school, rebuilt my first car engine before senior year, then decided to join the Army." When he met with a military recruiter, Slusher said that he wanted to work on cars and engines. "I signed up and have loved it ever since," he says.

For his first assignment, Slusher was sent to Germany, where he worked on a vehicle recovery team for four years. Slusher's inventory of recovery vehicles included the Heavy Expanded Mobility Tactical Truck, or HEMTT, a multipurpose vehicle manufactured by Oshkosh Truck that could be configured as a cargo carrier, fuel tanker, or wrecker. In addition, Slusher also drove the gigantic, 70-ton M88 armored recovery vehicle, designed for its crew to dislodge stuck vehicles and engage in repair activities — all while under fire in a combat zone.

At Ft. Riley, Slusher's current post of assignment, "We usually deal with a lot of breakdowns and bad engines," he says. In addition, he says, "every once in awhile we'll have a rollover, or someone getting stuck in the mud somewhere." HMMWVs, also known as high mobility multi-purpose wheeled vehicles or Humvees, originally lacked spare tire carriers. So a flat tire necessitated a tow, "usually with a five-ton wrecker like the M936A2," says Slusher. The M936A2, a 6-by-6 recovery vehicle, was eventually replaced with the MK36 wrecker.

Dewitt notes that his unit has six wreckers for rescuing disabled vehicles that weigh up to 10 tons. "Right now," he adds, "we're recovering mostly Humvees using light vehicle recovery procedures." In most cases, this involves towing a Humvee with another Humvee, using a towbar.

Larger vehicles require a recovery truck like the HEMTT M984A1, an 8-by-8, 10-ton wrecker with a main winch capacity of 30 tons. Additional equipment includes a self-recovery winch and a crane to assist in activities like lifting engines.

Then there are what are known as "tracked vehicles" like tanks, which when disabled require special recovery equipment. "For tracked vehicles we used to use an M88A1," says Slusher. "Now we have an updated model, the M88A2, also known as the Hercules." The newer versions of the M88 were redesigned to tow newer equipment like the M1A1 Abrams tank and the 52-ton Bradley fighting vehicle. Features of the M88A2 include a powerful 1050-horsepower V-12 engine, a 35-ton boom, a 70-ton main winch, and a three-ton auxiliary winch.

During an overseas deployment the Army recovery operator's job becomes even more important. Slusher was deployed to Iraq and typically used the HEMTT and five-ton wrecker in his work. He remembers one dangerous mission when he was called upon to rescue an MH-6 light attack helicopter that had been shot down. Slusher placed the small two-seat aircraft, affectionately known as "Little Bird," in the back of a light medium tactical vehicle (LMTV), a cargo carrier, and drove it off the battlefield. Later, Slusher recovered a Marine Corps troop transporter with his five-ton tow truck.

"When you're deployed," says Slusher, "you're usually dealing with accidents. And you still get your normal breakdowns and such. But there's more of a sense of urgency when you're deployed. You do whatever it takes to get disabled equipment out of the area." Danger is all around during a combat deployment, notes Slusher. "Soldiers' lives are on the line. The longer the equipment stays out there, the longer people have to stay to guard it."

Joshua Kohler was an Army Staff Sergeant assigned to the 445th

Transportation Company out of Waterloo, Iowa, when he was deployed to Iraq. While there, he and his fellow soldiers designated specific convoy vehicles to assist with recoveries. "We were using the Palletized Load System (PLS)" — a truck with removable cargo beds known as "flatracks" — "to recover Humvees and other disabled vehicles," Kohler recalls. "Each of our convoys was about 10 trucks long, and we would turn at least two of those trucks into recovery vehicles." The flatracks on those two PLS trucks were packed with spare tires, petroleum products, tow bars, cargo straps, and anything else that might be needed in the field.

By designating several of their vehicles to help with field repairs, the convoys were able to perform self-recoveries when needed — speeding up the process and keeping the convoy moving, which was critical in a combat zone. "If one of our trucks got a flat," continues Kohler, "we were able to fix it right on the road." One of the recovery PLS's would pull up next to the disabled vehicle and drop its tool-laden flatrack on the ground right next to it. Then the soldiers would get to work. "It made everything a lot faster," says Kohler.

How do Army mechanics and vehicle operators become recovery specialists? After attending basic training and Advanced Individual Training (AIT) to gain expertise in vehicle operations, the Army selects the top 10 percent of the class to attend its two-week vehicle recovery course at the Aberdeen Proving Ground in Maryland.

Army recovery specialists enter their career field for different reasons. Sergeant Dewitt, also assigned to the 101st Forward Support Battalion, grew up in Baltimore, Md., and wanted to stay close to his home and new wife. He attended a six-month course for track vehicle mechanics and then was chosen to follow up with recovery school.

Unlike the civilian towing industry, the military has a strict set of standard regulations that govern how vehicles are to be towed — and how the tow operators are to be trained for the job. "Different types of equipment have certain procedures you have to follow," says Dewitt. "Mostly it comes down to safety. You don't want someone who's not qualified to tow a certain piece of equipment because he or she can injure somebody else."

Whether a soldier operates an overhead lift crane, a troop transport vehicle, or a street cleaner, "the military ensures you've been properly trained on it," says Dewitt. Among other vehicles, he is certified to drive the M1A1 Abrams tank and the Bradley fighting vehicle. "A private might be certified on maybe one or two vehicles," says Dewitt. "By the time you're a Sergeant 1st Class, you need to know how to operate a lot of vehicles."

Those vehicles are typically parked in the military version of a tow yard, also known as the "motor pool." Equipment that is ready for use is staged on a ready line in an orderly fashion. According to Kohler, "we'd probably have them dress-right-dress, chock-blocked down. On the line in the motor pool is where we'd do our operator-level maintenance like changing tires, filling fluids, and checking oil, gas, air pressure, and battery levels." If a vehicle requires additional care, it is sent to the maintenance shop, which is either in or near the motor pool area.

Although military tow operators usually have little contact with their civilian counterparts, sometimes events will conspire to put the two together. In May 1997, the *New York Times* reported that a civilian towing company called on the military for assistance during a recovery operation on the Gowanus Expressway in Brooklyn. A 10-wheel truck packed with 12,000 pounds of bagged ice overturned on the highway, and the civilian towing company's conventional wrecker couldn't right the ice truck.

Meanwhile, a military tow truck from the Army's 101st Cavalry Division, traveling in the opposite direction, passed by the accident scene. The civilian tower flagged down the military heavy-duty vehicle, which lent its assistance, and the highway reopened for business three hours later. During that recovery operation, a little ingenuity and a lot of good timing made the difference. Although the customers and equipment might be different, civilian and military towers have the same mission: to recover a vehicle as quickly and as safely as possible.

Private Property Towing

Irate vehicle owners. Two truck drivers prowling for illegally parked cars. High impound fees. State laws that try to keep everything on an even keel. These are just some of the things that come to mind when people talk about private property towing. It can be a lucrative part of a towing company's repertoire, yet it can bring with it as many problems as profits.

Jeanette Rash, president of Fast Tow Wrecker Service in Houston, Texas, began conducting private property tows during the early 1980s. Her first contract was with a bank. To attend the nearby theatre, people would park their vehicles near the bank's ATM machines. With all the traffic, life became difficult for the bank's customers. "It was dangerous for the customers to get out of their cars to use the ATM machine just because someone else wanted covered parking," recalled Rash. "A little Triumph parked on their steps literally, too." Since the bank was responsible for the safety of its customers, it had Rash's company tow cars away from the ATMs.

However, private property towing isn't always such a dicey

proposition. In Oakland, Calif., Berry Brothers Towing & Transport, Inc., works as towing contractor for a number of local property owners, often via the security companies that are responsible for keeping watch over real estate such as large apartment buildings and condominium complexes. "Private property towing makes up about 10 to 15 percent of our impound business," said Bob Berry, whose company completed its first tow back in 1973.

A boxing match?

Because private property towing can be a legal minefield with angry vehicle owners complaining at every turn, some towers elect to keep their client base small. "Due to the negativity involved," explained Amanda Adolf, owner of Preferred Towing in Castaic, Calif., "we only conduct private property tows for a select few accounts."

Property owners and vehicle owners, sometimes glaring at each other with fists up, have varying opinions about private property towing. "Property owners are grateful for the service — removing an abandoned vehicle or a vehicle that's illegally parked," said Adolf. "Many vehicle owners knowingly park their vehicles in illegal areas, creating disorder and inconveniencing others."

While many vehicle owners act responsibly, some either don't understand or don't care about where they're leaving their vehicles. "For some reason, some vehicle owners feel they should be allowed to park or even abandon their vehicle wherever they want," noted Adolf. By the same token, she added, many vehicle owners do not clearly understand private property towing laws and tend to feel they have been victimized regardless of the circumstances.

Berry Brothers Towing makes signs that its property-owner clients can post around their real estate. It's important, said Berry, to make the rules clear to property owners. "In the state of California, if it's a retail outlet like a McDonald's, a 7-11, a grocery store or a shopping center, the car has to be there for at least an hour before it can be towed," explained Berry. The towers work with the property owner or the security company overseeing the premises. "We ask them to write down when the vehicle was first seen, and provide that information to us," said Berry. "We're required by law to put that down on our paperwork."

Parking lots and predators

Adolf finds that dealing with angry and out-of-control vehicle owners is one of the negative things about the job. "At times, vehicle owners feel they have been victimized and resort to violence," said Adolf, "never mind the fact that they disregarded the law and parked illegally."

Rash sympathizes with some of the parking companies in Houston, since their lots have often been the victims of customers who exit the premises without paying the fee. "They have many folks who just would not pay," explained Rash. Today, parking companies track their customers carefully, continued Rash, by noting the date, time and space of each vehicle. "It costs us all when people steal money from any company, including a parking company," added Rash.

Angry vehicle owners come in all shapes and sizes — and, sometimes, are even law enforcement officers. Rash notes that sometimes she has to tow patrol cars assigned to the county sheriff's department. "Some of them didn't pay as many as 20 times," she lamented. "One paid us in pennies one time to get us back. My clerk laughed and told the deputy that we needed change anyway — and made him stand by the window while she counted every single penny."

Unfortunately, towing companies can cause just as many problems as vehicle owners do. Predatory towers — those who look for a vehicle that may or may not be illegally parked, then charge exorbitant fees to release the vehicle to its owner — have made life difficult for towers who try to make an honest living. "There are some towing companies that do not adhere to the rules and regulations in regard to private property towing," said Adolf.

Adolf points to the television series "Operation Repo" as an example of how some companies, whatever their service, can paint an entire industry in horrible hues. "[The show] gives true repo companies a bad image," said Adolf. "'Operation Repo' is *not* real, but reenactments with paid actors." The show commonly depicts the repo company assaulting vehicle owners and entering private property illegally, said Adolf. Like the faux repossession team depicted in "Operation Repo," predatory towers have given the towing industry a poor reputation, explained Adolf: "I cannot express enough my disgust with predatory companies and the black eye it gives to the industry."

Local restrictions and how they affect a tower's business

Like other towers, Berry carefully follows state law when towing vehicles from private property. "We have over 2,500 accounts and we probably do on average two to three private property tows a day," said Berry. "We're really strict on the rules. We want to make sure we're not violating the law and exposing our customers — the property owners — to any liability. We try to keep them informed, and we ask that they stay informed about the law here in California."

In Texas, "we have a very, very good state law on private property towing," said Rash. However, she added, due to the prevalence of predatory towing in the state, towing companies need to be careful when dealing with the Texas Department of Licensing and Regulation (TDLR), which oversees the complaint process for vehicle owners who feel they've been improperly towed. "You may lose a tow hearing for no good reason," said Rash, "depending on the judge and if the people are convincing enough — even if you have photos."

"We are regulated to death now," continued Rash. "Previously we had good state laws but no enforcement. Now we have state enforcement, which is what we needed. But with all the heat from private property towing, we have local and county and state tow hearings. We may be dealing with several agencies about the same tow. It is wearing me out!" said Rash.

Similarly, in California, Adolf notes that a crackdown on predatory towing companies resulted in Vehicle Code Section 22658, which lays out regulations for private property towing. This includes fees, method of payment, notification requirements and the like. According to Adolf, one of the most notable cases in California ended in multiple charges filed against a towing company and its owners, who were eventually convicted of breaking the law. Unfortunately, that didn't stop these particular towers from preying on innocent motorists.

"These types of convictions should keep an individual from operating a towing company in the future; however, this is not the case," said Adolf. "The two owners are currently operating under a new company name listed to another individual in order to gain state contracts," she explained. "The new company is again conducting countless private property tows that may be in question." Adolf said that many vehicle owners have contacted her with questions about the new company and its efforts to tow vehicles from private property.

Adolf's frustration is echoed by other towers who feel that predatory towers are ruining the reputations of honest companies. "It is exactly these types of predatory towers that give the industry a black eye and cause new laws and regulations to be implemented," explained Adolf. "One bad apple spoils the barrel!" Laws that are meant to discourage predatory towing and protect vehicle owners, said Adolf, are often used in a manner not originally intended.

Rash points at predatory towers who tow even when signs are not posted or make use of "invisible or disappearing signs. It's baiting people," she said. "Why these bad towers just don't take the money and go down the road is beyond me. They have to get cash — which nowadays no one has on them — and they try to keep the cars to get an extra day of storage or other fees. It should be enough to just get the unwarranted tow bill and give people their cars back. But no, they have to pour salt on the wound."

Easing the pain

How do towers deal with angry vehicle owners who don't understand why their vehicles have been towed away? Adolf and her drivers provide a printout of the vehicle code section pertaining to their tow. "I make every attempt to explain the laws and regulations to all vehicle owners to ensure they understand why they were towed," said Adolf.

Rash recommends that towing companies make use of video and still photography: "I had to have it on video to protect my folks," she explained. "It has been a very good tool over many years."

"We take photos of each tow and we do our best to get the folks back on the road as quickly as possible with the least amount of hassle," said Rash, who makes heavy use of visual documentation. Her drivers take photographs of each tow to protect the towers as well as the vehicle owners. "I have video of the customers and the lot," said Rash. "We tell the customer that they are being videoed and we have a sign."

This watchfulness extends to Rash's staff as well. "I will fire an employee over being rude to a customer, no matter what," said Rash. "In more than one instance, the customer has said that my employee was rude but when I played the video back, the customer was the rude one."

Rash defends business owners who are simply trying to keep their property clean and in good working order. "You see trash and beer bottles scattered all around businesses that are located near nightclubs," noted Rash. "People see no reason to find restrooms and instead just go wherever in parking lots nearby." This requires the business to clean up its parking area every day, she said.

Given this, added Rash, it's only fair that businesses post "No Parking" signs and tow vehicles that appear on their lots illegally. "It's cheaper than hiring someone to clean up every day," she said, "and safer for the business so that it's less apt to get burglarized."

It's also important for towers to protect their businesses. One of Berry's personal rules about towing draws a clear line of demarcation between personal and professional issues when towing a vehicle: "I don't believe we should be involved in the *why* a vehicle is towed," said Berry, "just *how* it's towed and how it's stored and how much it [costs]."

Property owners, continued Berry, have the constitutional right to control access to their real estate. Towers are performing a contract service and need to be careful not to get embroiled in disputes. "It's not a lot different from dealing with police impounds," said Berry, "but it's a little more personal." Often the vehicle owner is having some type of problem with the property owner — a problem of which the tower is unaware until *after* the job is completed. Whether it's a dispute over a parking space or a property line, Berry and his drivers stay out of the middle of those relationships as much as possible.

Another way that Berry keeps his private property towing services clearly defined is by not doing any patrolling. "I don't think that's something a tow company needs to be involved in," he explained. "We provide a service to the property owner. When there's a problem, we're there and we'll provide quick and efficient service that complies with the law. Here again, Berry urges towers to stick to *how* a vehicle is towed, and not get involved in the *why*.

For all of its difficulties, private property towing is a valuable service to clients who want to keep their real estate in good shape. "The good thing about doing private property tows is ultimately keeping order," said Adolf. "Removing illegally parked vehicles and restoring order is necessary in many areas. When vehicle owners fail to read signs or knowingly park illegally it creates havoc." In the end, said Rash, it's a simple matter of respect for other people's property — and correcting the problem when someone fails to grant that respect.

The Thanksgiving Day Massacre

It's a story that involved city council members, parents, children — and a bunch of confused towers. Jeanette Rash, president of Fast Tow Wrecker Service in Houston, Texas, remembers a private property towing incident that occurred several years ago during the city's Thanksgiving Day parade. "My senior drivers know not to tow during the parade hours," said Rash. Unfortunately, she had a new driver on duty that day — a driver who was unaware of the rule.

The Mental Health Hospital has a parking lot that's reserved for its staff. "The employees of MHMRA (Mental Health and Mental Retardation Authority) work 24/7 like we do," noted Rash, "so they are in and out of the lot." During the parade, several unauthorized people parked their cars in reserved spots so they could attend the parade. Rash's new driver dutifully hooked up those illegally parked cars and towed them away.

Then things got sticky.

"I was at home cooking myself some dinner when my phone started ringing off the hook," recalled Rash. "Within 30 minutes I had three city council members who were in the parade call and ask me why in the Sam Hill we were towing people who came to see the parade."

The media pounced on the story: parents and their children were left without their vehicles. "It got all over the news and it was ugly!"

said Rash. The MHMRA staff informed the media that the hospital had ordered the towing so that its employees could get to work.

To smooth ruffled feathers, Rash had her drivers quickly return the impounded vehicles to their drivers. "Sometimes you just have to suck it up," said Rash. "Even if you are totally right, you have to think about the bigger picture."

Rash's fast action and her insistence on working with local officials have proven beneficial in the long run. "I had to make the best of it," she said. "And besides, kids were involved in this one."

Storage Facilities

Indoor or outdoor? Concealed or open to public view? Contract or non-contract? When a tow truck pulls a wrecked or impounded vehicle off the road, often its destination is the nearest storage area. Howard Sommers Towing, Inc., of Los Angeles boasts a versatile facility that can store approximately 650 vehicles indoors and many more in its expansive outdoor lot.

Overseeing this large towing firm is Robert Sommers, son of the company's founder. Since Howard Sommers Towing is a contract facility for the city of Los Angeles, the towing storage areas contain more than the typical wrecked cars and disabled vehicles.

"Within our indoor facility we have an investigative hold area," says Sommers. "There we store vehicles that are being held for law enforcement investigations. We separate those vehicles from everything else." The hold area features secure access and 24-hour video monitoring. In addition to vehicles marked for police investigation, Sommers' indoor area stores late-model and expensive cars for customers who want a safe place to park their property.

In Greenville, S.C., Mike Willimon, owner of Willimon's Auto Care, also has an indoor storage facility. This one has a capacity of up to 35 cars and, like Sommers' garage, exists primarily to hold vehicles tagged for police investigation. "We mainly store cars that are on hold for law enforcement," says Willimon, "along with cars that have a lot of value — high-dollar wheels."

Sommers' company is one of 17 towing firms contracted to the Los Angeles Police Department to tow and store vehicles at official police garages (OPGs). "There's a police garage in every division of the city," says Sommers. Over 200 recovery vehicles and 500 contract employees comprise the OPG system. Taken together, the contract storage facilities in the greater Los Angeles area stretch across more than 90 acres.

The city's towing and storage network wasn't always so highly organized, recalls Sommers. The current towing and storage system, utilizing a network of private contractors, was established in 1938 to handle the city's rapidly expanding road system. "Years earlier when the city created the official police garages, as a tower you had what was known as a 'designation.' As long as you did a good job, you had it as long as you wanted it."

Eventually the process became more formal, and the city put out a call for bids from local towing companies. In 1962, the city released a Request for Proposal (RFP) for contract towing and storage services. Approximately 75 different towing companies bid for the job. Howard Sommers Towing was awarded the contract for what's known as the West Valley division, a 52-square-mile area encompassing the western San Fernando Valley that includes over 750 miles of roadway.

In an arrangement familiar to most towers, Silverdale Towing of Silverdale, Wash., works with local law enforcement on a rotational basis, and picks up vehicles for storage when instructed to do so. According to Dispatch Manager Sheryl Therianos, "Our local 911 dispatch center takes care of the county and the different police forces," which include Kitsap County, Bainbridge Island and the cities of Poulsbo and Squamish. The state highway patrol handles its own dispatching, adds Therianos, but uses the same rotation list as the local police.

Since they often operate under contracts with local government agencies, many towing companies are required by local ordinance to provide a certain level of security on the premises. The city of Los Angeles, for example, has a set of stringent guidelines that contract towers must follow. "There's a list of do's and don'ts" that is "all-encompassing," says Sommers.

Because the city requires such diligence on the part of its contractors, Sommers feels that the added rules have helped improve the look and reputation of towing companies in general. "Instead of looking like a wrecking yard, we have a beautiful 35,000 square-foot warehouse and outdoor storage facility," he says. "Every space is numbered and coordinated. It helps expedite things, making it easier for people to get their vehicles out."

In addition to handling dispatch calls for the Los Angeles Police Department, official police garages like the one at Howard Sommers Towing juggle requests from the department of transportation and other city departments including the school district and the harbor and airport law enforcement units. The 17 official police garages in Los Angeles are responsible for covering 6,400 miles of streets, 40,000 intersections, and 160 miles of freeways.

With a colorful mix of wrecked, impounded and stored vehicles lined up row-by-row, tow yards can be an eyesore to drivers passing by. To remedy this issue, many local governments require a certain amount of camouflage around a storage area. In South Carolina, Willimon's Auto Care is required to conceal its storage facilities to a certain extent. "We have a city towing contract," says Mike Willimon, "so we have to have our fence blinded out. We also have a lighting system and closed-circuit cameras for security." In Los Angeles, the storage area for Howard Sommers Towing is enclosed in covered tennis-court fencing.

Meanwhile, at Silverdale Towing, Sheryl Therianos works out of an office in a lot surrounded by a chain-link fence topped with concertina wire — part of the city regulations for contract towers. "Our fence is covered with wood slats painted green," she says. "We also had to plant trees around most of our lot." The local zoning requirements also apply to the company's overflow lot six miles away, where Silverdale Towing holds periodic auctions on unclaimed vehicles.

ALLAN T. DUFFIN

Robert Sommers adds that some towing storage areas "look like a junkyard, and that's not what the cities want." He points to the lawn area, trees and flowers around his storage facility as an example of creative camouflage. "We look like any business," he says. "You don't see any junked or wrecked cars. Everything is hidden from view, even in our rear storage area." Sommers' facility also features hydraulically operated automobile racks for maximum storage capacity, plus an air evacuation system that can pump out 30,000 cubic feet of oxygen whenever the carbon monoxide levels inside the garage become too high.

On the other hand, sometimes there's little need for concealment and expensive security measures. In rural Rocky Mount, Mo., Gene Turpen's towing company is far off the beaten path. "I'm out in the country, a half-mile off my local highway," he says. Turpen maintains an outdoor storage yard with a capacity of 100 vehicles, which live on the premises in relative safety because, as Turpen says with a chuckle, "No one can see the vehicles to start with!"

Although a storage yard might be concealed from public view, Robert Sommers notes that the sharpness of the exterior should extend inside as well. With many people visiting storage firms to recover an impounded vehicle, for example, Sommers is well aware of the importance of solid customer service. "Everybody who comes into our place has a problem," he says. "They've been in an accident, their vehicle has been impounded, or something else has happened."

Sommers says that the city of Los Angeles "holds its drivers to a very high standard," which echoes the level of quality that his company sets for its employees. "We try to keep our trucks nice, neat and well maintained," he adds. "Our drivers go through additional training, plus safety training on a regular basis. We try to be a step above. As my dad taught me years ago, it's much cheaper to keep one man for 20 years than 20 men for one year."

According to Sommers, helpful customer service is even more critical when dealing with people whose vehicles have been towed or impounded, especially by local law enforcement authorities. "Try to help them," Sommers recommends. "Be kind to them. Maybe six months from now they'll break down and they'll remember that they were treated fairly at your facility. And maybe they'll call you for another tow." Good

144

word of mouth makes for great advertising, adds Sommers. "I give all my employees a bonus if they get a complimentary letter from a customer," he says.

In many ways, says Sommers, the relationship between towers and local law enforcement means that companies with storage facilities must pay close attention to public relations issues. As contract towers, "we represent the city," he explains. "We need to make a good impression so that the city leaves a good impression."

Building a Tower's Website

Call it "digital towing." The computer sitting on your desk can connect you with fellow towers around the world in the blink of an eye. And with a few clicks and some carefully chosen search words, you can find just about any information you need on the Internet. A Google search for towing companies or related information will uncover over 16 million Web pages of information. These days, many towers have a presence on the Internet, with at least one Web page that provides company data and contact information. Having your information easily accessible on the Internet in a "brochure"-type site can help boost your customer base significantly. But how are these sites created? And in the end, are they really that useful to towers?

Perhaps the greatest difference between towing sites and other business sites on the Internet is the time factor involved for most of the customers who visit the site. For example, to buy a pair of shoes you can visit a traditional "brick-and-mortar" store in your neighborhood or simply stay home and make your purchase online. On the other hand, if your right front tire just blew out and you're sitting on the shoulder calling for a tow, unless you have a mobile phone with wireless Web capability, you probably can't access the Internet to find the closest towing service.

Under more normal circumstances — for example, if you're at home searching for information about a towing company's equipment, or in your office trying to pay a purchase order by credit card — a Web site can make the process much easier. "Web sites give people an alternative to finding information and capabilities about our company," says Doug Harff, vice president of sales and marketing for United Road Towing, the largest towing company in the United States. "Along with direct mailings to our customers for awareness," he adds, "we can direct them to the Web site, where they can find more detailed information they need."

It's worthwhile to spend the money to market your company online, says Harff. "We posted our employment application so people can print it out. We posted job openings, held-for-sale assets, and lots of other information. The Web site helps broaden the base of people who might need our service." Harff works closely with a Web designer to keep www.unitedroadtowing.com up to date and useful for the firm's customers.

Another informative Web site is located at www.petrofftowing.com. Petroff Towing proudly calls itself "The Heavy Duty and Recovery Specialists of the Metro Saint Louis Area," and created a Web site that provides information about its four operating locations. Mixing a blue, gray and white color palette with dashboard-themed graphics, an energetic logo, and some background animation, the Petroff Web site is a good example of how to pack a lot of information into one place.

Petroff Towing didn't need to contract a web designer to create its site — Michelle Petroff built it herself, in-house. "I had previously worked for a company that did electronic publishing," she says, "so I came from a web design background." Petroff designed the original site for her family's company in 1998 and updated it in April of this year. In addition to brochure-type information, the site provides an online home for the racecars and drivers that the shop sponsors.

The simplest way to design and launch your Web site — and keep it up-to-date — is to hire a Web designer who can provide an all-inclusive package. Such a package can include the registration of a domain name, hosting of your Web site, the design itself, and ongoing updates and maintenance. By taking this route you need only pay one bill instead of several to keep your Web site going.

Your designer can be local if you prefer working face-to-face, but some towing firms hire designers from other states as well — sometimes on a referral from a trusted source, sometimes because the required expertise isn't available in the immediate area. Whatever approach you take, give the project your full attention, says Cheri Ellison-Carroll, owner of Ellison Towing, Inc., in Mountain View, Calif. "Nobody knows your company better than you do," she explains. "Set aside the time to work with your designer, and give him or her the content to make it happen."

When creating a new Web site, make sure that you clearly define the responsibilities of you and your designer, says Ellison-Carroll. "Is your Web designer going to take the photos for you? Who is going to think of catchy titles? You need to make sure that everything is clear." Towing firms that are searching for a designer need to do their homework, she says: "Take a look at the other Web sites they've done, and their most recent work. Also, know the true cost up front. If you see an existing Web site that you like, ask the designer how much it will cost to make a similar one for you."

Establishing a good working relationship with your designer is also critical to building a good Web site for your business. "You want to have somebody you really enjoy working with," says Ellison-Carroll, "because it really is a team effort." After you pay your designer for setting up the Web site, he or she can bill you periodically for any updates that you require. If your site needs frequent updating — for example, if you want to add fresh news every month about safety measures you're implementing in the shop, or if you want to post weekly photos of the latest recovery jobs — consider paying a monthly retainer fee to your designer. That way you know that he or she is ready to make updates whenever you request them.

Paying for individual updates can get expensive, so try to group your updates together. This also makes things easier for your Web designer. Also, remember that asking for major changes might necessitate a redesign of the site, which costs more. So when creating the initial design, try to allow for future expansion as much as possible.

Since fees vary by designer, make sure you discuss all of the pricing in detail before work begins on the site. Sometimes you can get deals on low-price (or even free) domain registration and hosting. Be careful about any "too-good-to-be-true" offers; review your designer's work samples and get things in writing. As with towing, sometimes those cheap prices mean you're getting so-so or substandard work.

Sometimes towing companies provide more than just general direction to their Web designers: they get involved in the layout of the site itself. At Ellison's Towing, Inc., Ellison-Carroll and her husband Brent contributed their creative skills to the project. "I worked with a company that created a lot of the formatting of the site," recalls Ellison-Carroll. "I did all of the writing, and Brent coordinated the photos. We worked on a lot of the design," which is accessible at www.ellisonstowing.com.

Whether you're creating a brand-new Web site or overhauling an existing one, here are some tips from designers and towers who have been through the process already:

Ask Yourself, "What's It All For?" This is the first and most important question for companies who want to build a Web site. What information will the Web site present to the customer, and what features will it have? "This is where we bring to the public what we work so hard to deliver," says Ellison-Carroll. Creating a Web site is a process of self-analysis, she adds. "It can be a wonderful experience because you get so much better acquainted with your own company." Answering basic questions about your business will help you design a Web site that is clear and helpful to the customer. "Ask yourself, 'Why are we so wonderful? What sets us apart?'" recommends Ellison-Carroll.

Branding. A good Web site is only part of a company's overall branding scheme. "Our Web site is part of our whole imaging campaign," says Petroff. The color scheme and logo displayed on the Web site carry over to the paint scheme on the company's equipment. "All of our trucks are blue with gray and chrome," notes Petroff. "Our Web colors complement that."

Domain name. The domain name for your Web site is usually your company name — for example, "johndoetowing.com." Your designer can check to see if the name is still available for use, since you'll need

150

to register it and pay an annual renewal fee. But once you've purchased the name, it's yours to keep. Just make sure that you pay your renewal fee each year. It's very similar to a magazine subscription. If your Web designer provides an all-inclusive service, then he or she will probably take care of this for you.

Hosting. Web sites typically consist of a series of "pages" and associated files — photos, graphics, forms, and the like — that are kept on a computer server. The company that provides server space to "host" your Web site will charge a fee for its service. Again, many web designers will include these fees in a package price for your Web site.

Design. Most "brochure" sites consist of a title, a few photos and some text. If you'd like to go a step further, hire a designer who has experience with graphic design. Web designers with an artistic edge over their peers can create layouts that break away from the basic, boxy, text-and-photo layout of most sites.

"Keep it clean and simple," recommends Michelle Petroff. "You need a good site map and navigation, with everything laid out logically." The site map is a flowchart of the site, showing how a visitor travels from one item to the next as he or she selects navigation buttons or pull-down menus. "A website needs a good flow from one item to the next," says Petroff. "The main things we wanted to feature included the types of equipment we use, all of our vendors, and the different types of services we offer."

At first glance, all of the information on a Web site might not be completely obvious. For her site, www.petrofftowing.com, Michelle Petroff included a wide variety of pages that are accessible only from the drop-down menu on the company's homepage. "There are lots of little hidden sections that you don't see at first," she says. "As you navigate the site, you can go layer by layer." This type of interactivity makes a visit to your site both interesting and fun for the customer.

Pricing. Designers charge anything from $99 into the thousands for a new Web site. The rate depends on the number of pages, complexity of the design, how soon you need the site completed, and the designer's experience. If you want animated features in your site, it will cost extra since it's additional programming work for the designer. Again, be aware that lower prices don't necessarily translate into good design, so be prepared to pay for good quality.

Plan for future expansion. Information and interactivity are important in creating a Web site that new and existing customers will visit again and again. "It's important to have an interactive Web site — and one you can grow with," says Ellison-Carroll, who recommends that towers consider including features like electronic forms and credit card processing on their sites. Providing online interactivity helps "bridge the sale" by making it easier for the customer, she adds.

Petroff Towing built a number of forward-looking features into its Web site. "We get visitors from all over the world," says Michelle Petroff. "And we get information requests not only from customers and towing enthusiasts, but also from towing companies across the globe." Among the site's visitors are towers from as far away as the United Kingdom, Australia and South Africa. The Petroff site allows visitors to create their own accounts and apply for credit as well. "Some customers contact us through the Web site," adds Petroff. "We can also do purchase orders online."

Doing it yourself. If you're creatively inclined and would rather design a site yourself, there are a number of software packages on the market that can speed the process along. Be aware of the cost, however: Adobe Dreamweaver (www.adobe.com/products/dreamweaver), one of the most widely used design programs, retails for $399. Freeway by Softpress (www.softpress.com), a Web design package specifically created for the Macintosh computer series, has a similar price tag. If you'd rather not dig into your budget for top-of-the-line design software, there are cheaper but less powerful design programs like CoffeeCup (www.coffeecup.com). Also, popular hosting services like Yahoo! offer very basic downloadable software packages that help you create a Web site quickly.

A sharp Web site is just one part of a towing firm's marketing strategy, albeit a critical one in this digital age. In fact, *not* having a Web site can actually hurt your business: technologically-minded customers might assume that if you're not up-to-date on the Web, then perhaps your equipment isn't either. Even a simple one-page Web site is better than no Web site at all. "We strive to maintain the highest standards of quality and professionalism," says Michelle Petroff, "and a Web site is yet another first impression of our business."

The Price of a Fill-Up

The country's current economic crunch is putting a crimp into the budgets of many businesses across the nation—and by extension the customers and families who depend on those businesses for products, services and paychecks. Towers are adding fuel surcharges and increasing their rates to keep their businesses up and running. But what about the human cost? How are higher fuel prices affecting the people who run the towing companies and drive the trucks? How are towers coping with an economic downturn that President Bush called "a difficult time for many American families"?

Curt Sharp, a tower from Grand Rapids. Mich., has heard from many operators around the country who are concerned with the higher cost of living and lower call volumes. "Unfortunately the economy is taking a beating right now, and it is difficult on every level," he says.

Towing expert George Bakker echoes Sharp's comments: "A lot of towing companies that I know of cut back on man hours, have closed down shifts, hired answering services where they used to have full-time dispatchers, cut their insurance rates, and are running equipment longer—rebuilding it, refurbishing it—just to try to weather the storm."

A flexible business plan may be the difference between staying busy and shutting down. "The efficiently run companies are weathering it a lot better," says Ralph Weber, a 10-year towing veteran who runs Route Three Life Health Disability, Inc. Route Three offers business planning, financial services and insurance planning for towers. "The evolution of the average tower goes like this: one man, one truck, and sometimes the spouse will take calls," explains Weber. In the beginning the business is not tremendously sophisticated, "but that comes with time." Those small companies, explains Weber, are the ones that hurt more during periods of economic strife.

By contrast, the average company—one with seven to 10 trucks— will weather the storm a bit better, says Weber. "They're able to pass on to most of their clients a fuel charge, or raise their rates. Everyone understands. They know it's going to cost more to send a UPS parcel. They know it's going to cost more to hail a cab. And they know it's going to cost more to hire a truck for towing."

Tightening the belt at home and at work

So far, employees are biting the bullet. According to Gary Coe, a former president of the Towing and Recovery Association of America and owner of Retriever Towing in Portland, Ore., "No one has called to say that they cannot afford the fuel to come to work. Certainly there are comments about prices in general, but no overwhelming effect." But at home, "people are going to be hard-pressed," says Bakker. Some items in the family budget—vacations, clothing and gifts, for example—will be scaled back or eliminated altogether.

Employees are keeping their supervisors apprised of their concerns at I-70 Towing and Recovery in Columbia, Mo. "Our employees' commute to work and back home is obviously making everyone complain," says Jennifer Furlong, dispatcher/secretary for the company. "The cost of fuel has made it difficult for all of us. I would say they are watching their spending habits more than ever."

Nick Schade hears the same concerns at his company, Tony's Wrecker Service, Inc., of Louisville, Ky. "Our employees are watching their pennies and not overspending. Discretionary spending is affected—people are postponing purchases instead of just going out and buying them." Schade has also noticed an uptick in employees' saving habits: "They're taking their paychecks, buying what they need, and saving the rest for a rainy day."

Tow company employees are also concerned about keeping their jobs. Coe is upbeat: "We certainly have no control over inflation," he says, "but we have not laid anyone off, so other than some higher costs of living, our people should not be affected unless we have a reduction in force." To keep going with an existing workforce, Sharp recommends that instead of hiring new employees, company owners consider adjusting schedules or adding responsibilities to their current staff.

The people around you

Towers who track their competitors' businesses gain a useful snapshot of how the economy is affecting their local area. On the outskirts of Louisville, Schade has seen fewer wreckers on the road. "But when I do see them," he says, "they're loaded. Gas might be $3.50 or $4.00 a gallon, but towing must go on."

To accommodate the rising cost of fuel, I-70 Towing instructed its staff to drive their trucks only for service calls. "We continually strive to dispatch our trucks promptly from one tow to the next, so unnecessary trips to the office and back out are eliminated," explains Furlong. Because the company's lot sits next door to the main office, Furlong tries to schedule meetings with insurance adjusters at the exact time a tow truck is bringing that car to the lot. This saves time and energy for everyone involved, and allows the company to focus on its main line of work: rescuing disabled vehicles.

At Tony's Wrecker Service, Schade lists a number of changes undertaken to combat the pitfalls of hard economic times: a slight increase in rates, stricter scheduling of services and doubling up on jobs. A tower might be dispatched as a two-car courier instead of sending two separate tow trucks to an accident scene. Sharp has observed some

157

interesting alliances forming in his Michigan town, including reluctant competitors working with each other and finding backhauls on long tows.

Businesses that support the towing industry are also combating the effects of a faltering economy. "We have seen fuel surcharges from the laundry company and several parts suppliers," says Coe. "Everyone is affected." Coe notes that his customers have been understanding about the all-around increase in prices: "Customers aren't complaining about the surcharge. They know what's going on. They all go to the gas pumps too."

Some towers continue to gain additional business. For example, I-70 Towing recently won a major local contract. "It's with the University of Missouri," says Furlong. For their small-truck business, this should ensure mor ework for the team—"and that means more money in their pockets," she adds.

Purchasing more equipment?

Can business owners afford to replace worn out equipment or purchase new trucks? "There are many companies suffering," says Furlong, "not justthe towingindustry." She notes that severallarge truck lines that have been forced toreturn their leased trucks to the dealershipsdue to therising cost of fuel.

But for the towers we talked to, things aren't quite so bad. "When we are busy, we wear out trucks," says Coe matter-of-factly. "So there is no effect on my plans to replace equipment as needed." Furlong agrees: "We're the fastest-growing tow company in central Missouri," she says. "We just added another light-duty truck to our fleet in early July." Schade recently purchased a new rotator for his company.

One might assume that in a slow economy, business slows down as well. According to news reports, to save on fuel costs, many people are driving less. But despite reduced traffic on the roads, Coe reports that his business has actually increased. Why?

"When fuel prices are up, people hang onto their cars longer," explains Weber. "The older the car, the more it breaks down. That helps balance things out." In a good economy, a car owner might trade in his or her vehicle every three years, he says. If the economy is bad, older cars are no longer covered by the manufacturer's warranties. In addition, when the cost of gas increases, vehicle owners delay making repairs. This means higher call volumes for towers when older cars break down. "The towing industry's success rate has always been an inverse to the state of the economy," explains Weber. "So when the economy is bad, our business picks up."

Future plans

In such an unpredictable economic climate, how can towers plan ahead? "I think a lot of companies will be trying to figure out ways to be more efficient," says Furlong. "This will be better for fuel prices and, of course, the management of our businesses."

Schade notes that continued aggressive advertising is important during the economic downturn. "We're still working at our steady pace, still continuing to market our services, making our calls like we're supposed to," he says. "We need to let people know we're still there and still moving." Schade says that a strong marketing push can help his company pick up any slack from other towing businesses that have cut back or closed their doors.

Coe regularly monitors the additional cost of fuel against a two-year baseline and against revenue from the fuel surcharge. "We want to make certain that we are keeping up with the additional cost, yet not taking advantage of our customers."

Sharp cautions that towers need to plan ahead, since quick reactions to the current economy might only serve as band-aids rather than permanent solutions. "While raising rates, fuel surcharges, budget cuts, and the like may help ease the pain temporarily, we need to start making large long-term plans to protect our businesses," he urges. To get started, Sharp offers the following thoughts:

—Are you buying the fuel at the best price that you can? Check the local gas stations, commercial fueling locations, and bulk fuel suppliers and do some number crunching.

—Take a good look at your entire budget. Is there fat that can be trimmed?

ALLAN T. DUFFIN

— Have you considered Bio-Diesel that may be less expensive, or hydrogen systems that can increase fuel economy?

— Do you maintain proper tire inflation and mechanical care of your trucks? The next time you purchase tires, talk with your supplier about fuel economy. Most tire manufacturers will have study data that compares the different tire compounds and tread designs. Is that deep mud/snow lug tire really the best purchase when you come to realize that you are only in mud or snow for 20 percent of your mileage?

— Tighten the reins a little on dispatching. Do you save much time by sending the next driver 15 miles across town when you may have another truck clear in the area in 30 minutes, or are you just donating fuel to the cause? Customer ETAs are important, but so is operating a sound business that will be here in 10 years.

— Review the types of calls that you actually run. Sometimes there may be a difference in the type of calls that your company is running and the type of calls that you think you are running. This will give you a better idea of your future needs.

— Do you need a new flatbed? Yes, I know that your call volume has picked up and your trucks are busy. But what are they busy doing? What percentage of your calls are service calls? Maybe the purchase of a small pick-up would serve you better as a service truck—and for a lot less money, better fuel mileage and lower insurance.

— Invest in operator/dispatcher training. How many times have we seen or heard drivers requesting a flatbed because the disabled vehicle is an AWD, or a wheel-lift truck because the vehicle is stuck in park? We will never get completely away from this; however, it's important to ask the right questions when the customer is on the phone, and to train your operators in different methods of handling the difficult calls. While all of this may seem small now, sending the wrong truck 10 miles across town and back can cost $10.00 in fuel alone!

Sharp realizes that some of these notes might work better for larger companies that two-truck operators, "but the idea is to take a good hard look at your actual business plan and prepare you for the long haul," he

160

explains. "As industry professionals, we owe it to our customers and to ourselves to find new business practices to help control costs."

In the end, adjusting to the country's rollercoaster economy can help sharpen a towing company's efficiency—for management and for the workforce. "I feel that our employees are making better decisions and making sacrifices in other areas to ensure that they make ends meet," says Furlong, adding that her company is more focused than ever on its core business. Despite some increased costs, "We still make sure that customer service is our first priority," she says.

Towing companies will weather the economic storm as they always have. Getting through it won't be easy, but a watchful eye and a careful plan will help towers stay afloat. After all, says Schade, "Towing will stay here, and we will too."

Crashing Real Estate Tows Away Business

The rise in fuel prices, combined with the downturn in the real estate market, has put a crimp in the towing business in some vacation cities and wealthy resort areas.

Cities like Miami, Fla., are experiencing difficult economic situations. "Times are very tough for the average Miamian due to the real estate market and fuel prices," says Janie Coffey, owner of Papillon Real Estate LLC, a boutique brokerage based in Coral Gables, Fla. "An oversupply of luxury condos were (and still are being) built which did not have the supply of actual residents (owners or renters)," she adds. "Speculative 'investors' bought as greedy developers looked the other way, then when the market crashed, the 'investors' walked away leaving building after luxury building empty or, worse, in receivership."

In Naples, a city in southwest Florida whose economy relies primarily on tourism, high fuel prices and a crashing real estate market are making things difficult for local towers. "Real estate has been really hot here," says Doug Young of Bumper to Bumper Towing. "That's really the only industry we have—building residential and commercial real estate, shopping centers, banks, high-end homes and condos." For the past decade, adds Young, "this place has been growing as fast as they can build it." Dump trucks, concrete trucks and supply trucks were a regular part of the landscape.

Then the bottom fell out of the real estate market. "It was a mass building project and it's all come to a complete stop," notes Young. With the number of construction and personal vehicles dwindling, there was little left to tow. "It's affected the guys who do heavy towing a lot," says Young," and even the people doing the smaller, rollback tows. The people aren't here. They're just not driving on the road. So the number of accidents has gone down dramatically."

Another regular source of business that has nearly disappeared came from the Naples police department. Young says that many migrant workers have left the city due to lack of employment. "They were constantly getting arrested and having problems with their drivers licenses and plates," he explains. Companies like Young's were busy responding to police calls to tow vehicles. But with the exodus of workers due to the sagging economy, those police calls have decreased dramatically.

What about a tourist spot like Las Vegas, where sales of luxury homes have fallen by more than 50 percent? "The credit crunch is affecting all market segments," writes Brian Wargo in a recent article in the *Las Vegas Sun*, "and pressure has tightened the most for high-end loans, analysts said. That is taking a lot of buyers out of the marketplace."

Despite the housing market crash in Vegas, Bobby Howell, vice president and owner of AA Action Towing, Inc., actually reports an *increase* in business. Part of the reason is that the company's regular client base has remained relatively stable over time. "We've been in town for 22 years," says Howell. "Summertime is always our busiest time of the year because of the heat." But why are Howell's numbers up in a down market? Unlike the situation in Naples, Fla., the city of Las Vegas isn't built primarily on housing construction. "Vegas is Vegas," says Howell. "People are always going to come here."

State of the Industry with David Beer

A perfect safety record. Dual businesses in towing and collision repair. Twenty-eight years as the president of his own company. David Beer, a TRAA Level 1 certified tower and the owner of Five Seasons Auto Rebuilders in Cedar Rapids, Iowa, has seen a lot during his time in the industry. His high standards have paid off: Five Seasons has received customer recognition awards from motor clubs in addition to several American Towman ACE Awards for achievement in service performance.

Beer started in the business as a teenager. Fresh out of high school, he attended a trade school to learn collision repair. After working at a repair facility for a short period, he quickly realized that he wanted to be his own boss. In July 1981 he opened Five Seasons Auto Rebuilders.

The business took off quickly. "We started out as strictly a collision repair facility, then branched out into towing," says Beer. Initially the towing side of the business existed to help keep the collision repair facility busy. "But we found out quickly that our towing business was growing as quickly as collision repair," he recalls. "Towing took on its own identity."

One truck, fewer services?

Towers often start out small and slowly, growing their businesses over time. With steady guidance and attention to standards, towing companies can build strong reputations and succeed in a highly competitive industry. Unfortunately, this isn't always the case. Some tow truck operators launch their businesses literally from their own garages — with less than stellar results. Beer notes that during the last year or two, motor clubs seem to be getting more comfortable with using contractors that have just one or two trucks. Often these tow truck operators work out of their homes.

"It's very hard to compete with companies like that because their overhead is so low," says Beer. However, he adds, tiny towing companies also have a definite disadvantage in that they lack the assets or ability to respond to multiple, overlapping jobs in a timely manner. It can be difficult if not impossible to handle work for different municipalities and various commercial accounts at the same time. "They can do one, maybe two — if they're lucky — recoveries at a time," explains Beer. Moreover, he says, one-truck firms don't have the resources to ensure that their employees have the right training.

Although this issue can cause larger towing companies a lot of heartache, Beer acknowledges that things look different from the auto clubs' point of view. "They're looking at the big picture," says Beer. "They're thinking, 'We can get services for 'X' dollars from a major towing company, but we can get the same services for 20 percent less from a smaller company.'"

When small towing companies are moved to the primary position on a motor club's list of contractors, larger towers are relegated to second position, explains Beer. This situation continues until the smaller companies can't handle the workload and the motor club is forced to move up to a larger towing firm.

Automakers and decline in dealerships

With regard to motor clubs and their contracts with towers, Beer has seen a number of changes over the last several years — changes exacerbated by today's difficult economy. "With Chrysler, for example, we've seen a steady decline of benefits," says Beer. "Fifteen years ago Chrysler paid for just about anything — door unlocks, jumpstarts, everything. We could go anywhere in the state and be fairly well assured that the call would be covered." As time has moved on, however, Beer has seen fewer and fewer benefits provided to the customer. Unlocking doors, for example, was removed from the benefits list "quite some time ago," he says.

These developments have trickled down to the towing industry. With fewer benefits offered to the customer, towing companies don't get those calls any more. It's an ironic situation, says Beer: "Toyota, for example, has TV commercials that say their cars are more reliable mechanically. Yet at the same time they offer few services as a motor club for their cars."

On the other hand, Beer notes that General Motors — which, like Chrysler, is currently undergoing bankruptcy proceedings — offers "fantastic" benefits for roadside assistance. That, however, might be changing. In May, Chrysler announced its plans to shut down 789 of its 3,200 dealerships in the United States. The Associated Press quoted Chrysler as saying "that the [dealership] network is antiquated and has too many stores competing with each other" and that "many of the dealers' sales are too low." Meanwhile, General Motors contacted 1,100 dealerships to let them know that they were getting the axe.

Though he pays close attention to what's happening with vehicle manufacturers, the decline in dealerships hasn't affected Beer's company much. "Having been in business for 30 years we've seen a lot of dealerships come and go," says Beer. "Part of the reason is that dealership service facilities don't necessarily look for the best tower." Instead, he explains, dealerships are more inclined to call someone familiar — a buddy or a friend — to handle towing jobs. "Consequently all that work goes to people who are friends of the service advisors," says Beer, "so it really doesn't affect us."

Insurance companies and motor clubs

Beer has noticed that insurance companies are swiftly gaining more control with regard to the towing of damaged vehicles — something he predicted would happen a decade ago as he worked collision repair jobs. "Insurance companies are now pushing motor clubs to become a direct 'repair funnel,'" says Beer. When a tower picks up a car at an accident scene, the insurance companies make sure that the vehicle goes directly to a contract repair facility, rather than to a garage or impound lot.

"They want the car to go directly to the repair facility that the insurance company contracts with to do repairs," explains Beer. As an example he cites Allied, a blue ribbon shop and direct repair facility available to clients through an insurance company's Direct Repair Program, or DRP. Clients who select the DRP option in their policies can take damaged vehicles to an authorized repair facility.

Due to this new trend, sometimes the towing companies get caught in the middle. Beer recalls receiving a recent accident call for one of the motor clubs. "They indicated what repair shop to go to at dispatch," he says. However, the customer changed his mind and told the tow truck driver that he wanted to take his vehicle to a different repair shop.

"Within an hour I got calls from the insurance company and the motor club representatives," says Beer. "They were very unhappy with us that the car went somewhere else." Unfortunately there was little that Beer could do. "It was the customer's car, and he chose to have it towed somewhere else," says Beer. "The customer does own his vehicle, and he has the right to go wherever he wants."

Regarding contracts in general, Beer expresses some frustration over how they're bid and awarded. The problem with municipal, law enforcement, state and county contracts, he says, is that they can lend themselves to ethically questionable behavior. "People in law enforcement or city municipalities tend to want to make sure their friend has the contract, rather than the guy they think will do the best job," says Beer. "In 30 years I haven't seen a fairly bid municipal contract in our area."

Why does this happen? "In Cedar Rapids, towing is treated as a cash cow," he explains. "Our municipality charges a city administrative fee for towing that is more than the contract bid price and gives nothing back to the industry." Beer maintains that the local government "is fixated on a single-tower award with no tower input. Under our single-bid tower contract, if you complain, you're disqualified," he explains.

With this in mind, Beer typically avoids bidding on municipal contracts in his area "because they're so difficult to get and keep." People who are charged with enforcing the rules and standards of the contracts, he adds, have a difficult job because the standards are almost unrealistic, "and they only enforce them when they want to."

Things to keep in mind

Over the years Beer has collected a number of tenets that guide him in his business. "Succeeding in this industry takes a delicate balance of business savvy — of keeping our trucks rolling while at the same time conducting business in a workmanlike manner," he says.

Beer has seen his share of unprofessional behavior in the industry, but is heartened to see many towers who do their jobs with pride and high standards. "I'd like the industry to get to the point where it's less critical of itself," says Beer, "and polices itself in a professional manner rather than trying to undercut the next guy." Such cooperation and self-evaluation, he explains, will benefit every towing company, large or small.

Moreover, Beer feels that the services provided by towing companies are extremely undervalued. "How often, if you call any service at three in the morning, can you get anything for $50? That's a good deal!" And, he adds, many motor clubs are paying towers less than $50 — 30 to 50 percent less, in fact. "I realize that this is a business and that you don't always have to be appreciated for what you do, but our services are definitely undervalued."

By the same token, says Beer, towers need to ensure that they recognize their own value as well. "If, for example, we choose to work for rates that are less than the cost of production, it's our own fault." Setting the bar high is important as towers look to the future. "It's our industry," notes Beer. "As tow truck owners and operators, it's our choice what we allow in the industry."

Dealerships down, business up?

The bankruptcy of automakers like Chrysler and General Motors, and the subsequent closing of multiple auto dealerships to cut costs, affects every company affiliated with these businesses — parts suppliers, equipment manufacturers and motor clubs, to name several. But instead of seeing their business worsen as major automakers suffer through crisis after crisis, several national motor clubs report that they're actually experiencing growth.

Cross Country Automotive Services, based in Medford, Mass., is the motor club contractor for General Motors. How is the automaker's recent bankruptcy announcement affecting Cross Country's business? As it turns out, not much at all. "Our business is diversified in terms of clients and services, which gives us stability," says Amy Villeneuve, executive vice president of marketing, strategy and product innovation.

Villeneueve sees Cross Country's customer base increasing rather than decreasing. "We're actually adding auto and insurance customers because they increasingly see the value of our contact with their customers," she explains. "It comes down to providing real value at a time when the average age of a vehicle on the road is rising and the tough economy is forcing many folks to put off or delay new vehicle purchases."

Cross Country's emphasis on promoting good value is also important, says Charlie Cavolina, senior vice president of service delivery. "In fact, we're in the process of introducing a discount program for our service providers. We want to thank them and provide added value in a down economy, so we're working with major brands to get discounts on fuel cards, tow parts, uniforms, health care, phone service — even trucks."

In Clearwater, Fla., AutoLoop, and the hundreds of dealerships it services, are seeing an uptick in business — at a rate of 15 percent each month — during one of the worst economic times in America's history. "We're growing because we're effectively helping dealerships drive more customer attention to their stores," says Steve Anderson, president of AutoLoop. That customer attention is critical, he explains, because dealerships are selling fewer cars in a down economy.

Anderson notes that more vehicles are getting serviced these days because of fewer trade-ins and increasing vehicle age. By using a marketing system that automates e-mail reminders, text messages, interactive voice calls and print media, Anderson says that AutoLoop helps boost dealer business "in a way that doesn't require effort from the dealership itself."

Anderson explains that dealerships are coming to AutoLoop in part because the cost is low, and their ROI (return-on-investment) reporting is so in-depth. AutoLoop's automated marketing and reporting, says

Anderson, gives the dealerships a way to "strategically bring their customers back without having to hire more personnel."

So why are these dealerships seeing a boost in business in an economic environment where the opposite is expected? Anderson points to his company's use of proprietary technology. Because of that, "we don't really do much marketing," he says. "Almost all of our growth is through word of mouth and referrals because of how effective our whole system is." Says Villeneueve: "Our job is to keep looking — and finding — new and innovative ways to be of value to everybody: drivers, automakers, and service providers."

Overweight and Underappreciated: H.R. 1451 and the Weight Exemption Rule

Heavy-duty tow truck operators might have some legal assistance coming to them down the road. House Resolution 1451 might sound simple but, if enacted into law, could have wide-reaching effects on the towing industry.

Sponsored by Pennsylvania Rep. William Shuster of Pennsylvania's 9th District, H.R. 1451 proposes an amendment to Title 23 of the U.S. Code, allowing for an exception to weight limits on particular types of tow truck. Rep. Robert Brady of Pennsylvania's 1st District is the bill's co-sponsor.

What does the bill propose to do? Heavy-duty towers that transport Class 8 casualty vehicles — those weighing over 33,000 pounds — would be given an exemption from federal weight limits on their tow trucks, allowing the towers to use trucks weighing more than the currently allowable 150,000 pounds. The tower could then transport the casualty vehicle on the interstate highway system to a storage or repair facility at a distance of up to 100 miles from the recovery point.

Oshkosh Corporation and Jerr-Dan Corporation lobbied for the bill to help heavy-duty towers. John Daggett, director of communications for Oshkosh, provided a copy of the company's one-sheet about this issue. The current problem, according to Oshkosh, is that "once these tow trucks leave the immediate accident locations with casualty vehicles attached, the tow trucks no longer conform to rear axle weight limitation laws."

Because of this, heavy-duty towers get in trouble once they hook up the casualty and depart the accident location. Suddenly the towers are driving heavy and are in danger of being hit with fines for completing a job that was might have been ordered by local authorities in the first place.

This is a massive Catch-22 — Federal law that often increases the problem it's supposed to solve. H.R. 1451 proposes to alleviate that issue. "State and federal enforcement agencies have placed significant equipment demands on contract tow operators to minimize road closures and other hazards presented by disabled vehicles," writes Oshkosh, "yet these agencies later penalize the same operators at the scale house, or during traffic stops with portable scales."

Notwithstanding the weight of the towing vehicle, the weight of the *casualty* vehicle can be staggering. "When you look at a normal tractor trailer you're looking at 12,000 pounds on the steer axle on the cab, 34,000 pounds on the front tandem axles, and 34,000 pounds on the rear tandem axles, which makes 80,000 pounds," explains Hawkins. "That's where the term '18-wheeler' comes from," he adds — 10 wheels on the cab and another eight wheels on the trailer.

In an attempt to get around the problem and still do their jobs, some towers take dangerous risks: They use recovery vehicles that are "too short in wheelbase length, under capacity in equipment strength, light in axle capability, and overall too small to safely handle the weight of Class 8 truck casualties," points out Oshkosh.

Plain-vanilla solutions?

With this in mind, H.R. 1451 proposes resetting Federal standards and treating tow trucks as emergency vehicles, as well as improving communications between law enforcement authorities and weigh station operators. But the bill, say towers, won't take care of the entire problem.

"I think the bill in its present state is a good basic start," says Earl Mumma, president of Highspire Auto & Truck Repair Corporation in Steelton, Penn. Mumma has heard complaints from towers who say they need laws that allow some leeway in transporting casualty vehicles on interstates and secondary roads. Mumma tries to balance the practical side of things with the business needs of towers: "I feel the industry needs to keep in mind this is an incident management tool to clear freeways, not to make towers more money," he explains.

John Hawkins, vice president of sales for Miller Industries, says that banding together in pursuit of a purpose can result in huge changes for towers across the nation. Hawkins has been a big proponent of citizen advocacy since he entered the towing industry three decades ago. "When I started in this business in 1976 with my father, we sat down with a group of towers to talk about how as a group they had rights."

That discussion eventually led to the formation of the Professional Wrecker Operators of Florida, which was incorporated in 1977 as a membership group that wanted to boost working conditions, profitability and the overall image of the towing industry. Hawkins believed so strongly that he initially funded the group out of his own pocket. "This is how our system works," says Hawkins. "Through the constituents within a state. I believe in going to the state capitol and getting things done for the industry." Today the organization has approximately 300 members and employs a full-time executive director and staff with a lobbyist to push towers' concerns at the state level.

Despite his faith in the power of politics, Hawkins has concerns about H.R. 1451. "I think it's extremely vanilla and generic," he says. But Hawkins is quick to point out that the bill is a definite step in the right direction for the towing industry. "I don't mean to diminish or take anything away from what people have done," he says. "As a major manufacturer I should work hard to give our customers a vehicle that has legitimate ratings and legitimate capacities, but I should also work hard to maximize the payload that the customer can carry with my unit. If I have no reason to do that — if you just say in your bill, 'Okay, tow truck, you're exempt' — that can be dangerous. Because then we're causing damage to bridges and roadways, and we're adding to just cause."

Hawkins wonders which is better: getting something passed now, or continuing to massage the bill until it's just right. "If H.R. 1451 becomes adopted as written, is it good or bad? That would bemy question, and one admittedly I do not know the answer to.If weas an industry come back later to add further legislation, the Congressional committee might say, 'Hey, we just gave this industry a reprieve, and now they're coming back for more.' So is it right to leave [the bill] as written and then come back later, or is it better to get it right first? I guess that's why they call it politics!"

Scott Burrows, president of Burrows Wrecker Service in Pendleton, Ky., also sees H.R. 1451 as a step in the right direction, but notes that there are still many issues that need to be clarified. "For example," he says, "while addressing the weight issue, it leaves unanswered the question of what is an 'appropriate destination' open to interpretation by the enforcement agency."

Hawkins is also concerned that although there's been much discussion about problems that towers have encountered at weigh stations, H.R. 1451 doesn't really address how weighing procedures should be standardized. "I can pull into one scale and the gentleman who's been weighing vehicles for 30 or 40 years will look at me and say, 'Go'," says Hawkins. "But I can go to the next scale, where another gentleman who's also been doing the job for 30 or 40 years might tell me that my weight is unacceptable under this new statute."

Combination vehicles

If the bill makes it into law, says Burrows, it would be important to add language that would overlook the "over-length" of combination vehicles being towed behind long-wheelbase tow trucks. Without this additional exemption, explains Burrows, an overzealous enforcement official will have additional opportunities to cite tow operators for violations.

Brian Bolus, president of Minuteman Towing & Repairs, Inc., in Mifflinville, Penn., feels so strongly about H.R. 1451 that he visited his congressman in Washington, D.C., to discuss the proposed bill. Bolus' operations manager, Paul Johnson, sees the bill as helpful to the towing industry but, like Burrows, is concerned about requirements for combination vehicles.

"The bill does not include combinations," says Johnson. "Combinations should be included, either by a definition of disabled vehicle or as a specific item. As we know, for reasons of public safety, many combinations cannot be safely or practically split along the side of the road."

Johnson notes that poor shoulder conditions — soft, uneven and poor grading, to name several — along with inadequate or damaged landing gear, low fifth wheels, and hazardous cargo are only a few of the reasons why it's not good public policy to split combinations along interstate highways.

"Another compelling reason," continues Johnson, "is that the additional time needed to split a combination extends the duration of an incident, thus exposing the public to greater risk of secondary accidents and their associated deaths, injuries and property damage. (Secondary accidents are the cause of one in seven highway deaths, says Johnson.)

State-by-state

While H.R. 1451 addresses towing operations along interstate highway systems, it doesn't mention what happens to a tower who drives through different government jurisdictions: What if the tower crosses from federal onto state or county roads on his trip to the repair facility? "The bill talks about a repair facility within 100 miles, but who defines that?" asks Hawkins. "Who defines what our safe harbor is? If you go to Oregon it's 75 miles. But it's different in other states."

Also missing from the bill is a provision for permitted loads to deviate from their route due to unanticipated repairs, says Johnson. Requiring a tow truck to obtain a new permit will cause additional delays and associated risks.

In addition, H.R. 1451 does not exempt over-length vehicles. In

Pennsylvania — where the bill originated — disabled vehicles towed by a wrecker are already exempt from length limits. "The long wheelbases of our large wreckers, while creating a very long combination, help control road and bridge overload by spreading the weight of each of the combination vehicles over a longer surface area," explains Johnson.

Hawkins also notes that axle weight is crucial. "If we expect to get anywhere on the national or state level, we have to meet certain guidelines for what an axle can weigh," he says. "In most states that number is 20,000 pounds."

On the other hand, he says, the vast majority of states target 34,000 pounds on the drive axles if a tower is pulling a disabled vehicle. "In some situations that's okay," says Hawkins. The heavy-duty tower's biggest challenge, he explains, is in "big-fixed frame vehicles" — mixers, pumpers, fire engines, cranes, drilling units — that can have up to four or five axles. "The front end weighs in excess of 16, 18, or 20,000 pounds," explains Hawkins.

When these fixed frame vehicles break down, "that's really where the problem comes in," cautions Hawkins. "You takethese vehiclesand you have to tow them." This is what a bill like H.R. 1451 needs to define, he says. "This is our industry's current challenge: disabled vehicles that we cannot break down in order to reduce overall weight and height," he explains. "So this type of disabled vehicle has to be legal by itself, or is traveling with a permit." Either way, adds Hawkins, the vehicle "needs a secure home off the roadway after becoming disabled."

Johnson feels that wreckers towing in excess of 80,000 pounds should be required to purchase an annual permit from either the state or the U.S. Department of Transportation. "This permit should be of nominal cost, $50 to $100," he says, "and should require that any truck applying for such a permit be safely capable of handling such a load. This would eliminate the fear that many have articulated of F350s towing large combinations," explains Johnson.

If a move to increase legal weights to 98,000 pounds materializes, as Johnson says many forecast it will, the 150,000 pound combination limit still might not be enough to allow an adequately sized wrecker to tow one of these units off the highway.

For these reasons and more, finding a solution is a dicey proposition.

Perhaps Hawkins says it best: "There's no consistency and that becomes the challenge."

Looking down the road

Back on Capitol Hill, H.R. 1451 has been "in committee" for a long time. Mumma cautions that compromise and collaboration are necessary to see the bill through the legislative process. "The towing industry doesn't have a large lobby and is fragmented in their approach," he explains. "If the bill gets attacked by the very industry that needs it, the bill will be doomed to failure."

Burrows agrees that getting the bill passed will be an uphill battle. "Towers will not see a 'one-size-fits-all' bill in Congress," he says. "There are too many jurisdictions, too many other regulatory entities, and too little funding to see meaningful legislation make its way through both houses of Congress and the White House."

In the same vein, Johnson is concerned about how seriously Congress is taking the proposal. "I don't think it was proposed as legislation to be passed, but rather to pacify someone," he says. "No one in Rep. Shuster's office has any knowledge of the bill, why it was introduced, or other relevant information that one would expect them to have if it were a serious issue," says a frustrated Johnson. "I don't know if a groundswell of comment from our industry, as well as the trucking industry, would bring this bill to serious consideration."

On the other hand, Johnson sees the bill as a critical piece of leverage for towers everywhere. "Our industry, with the help of the trucking industry that we service, needs to use H.R. 1451 as a common starting point to convince our federal and state legislators that there needs to be a way to legally tow all the vehicles that they license and permit from the highways in the event of emergencies and breakdowns."

Despite the problems inherent in getting H.R. 1451 enacted into federal law, "I commend the folks that are trying to move this forward," says Mumma. "All legislation is an uphill battle."

Better Billing

In these difficult economic times, properly and effectively billing a customer for a recovery job is more important than ever. "I see many towers cutting prices," says Earl Mumma, president of Highspire Auto & Truck Repair Corporation in Steelton, Penn. "Remember when you hook up, your company is on the line — and maybe your home and future," urges Mumma. "Be careful!"

Also working to give their customers good service and fair billing are road service companies — "motor clubs" of sorts — that centralize the business by serving as a one-stop shop for towing and maintenance needs for truck and vehicle fleets. But the growth of these companies has caused heated debate in the towing community. What are the most effective ways to bill customers? And are road service companies helping or hurting the industry by consolidating so many towing businesses under one umbrella?

Reviewing the bills

Organizations like the American Towing Alliance, or ATA, have created nationwide networks of towing companies whose efforts are coordinated through a central location. ATA's operations, for example, are based out of its corporate office in Upland, Calif. The company was formed in 2001 and was endorsed by the American Trucking Association in 2004 when their membership expressed concern about how some heavy-duty towing companies were overbilling truckers.

President and COO Chris Carlson, a former aerospace engineer and operations consultant, founded ATA with two Southern California heavy towers including Danny Meister, a 30-year industry veteran and owner of Freddie Mac's Towing in South El Monte, Calif. "We saw a need to bring the best heavy towers together to serve Class 8 fleets on a nationwide basis," explains Carlson.

At Cherryville, N.C.-based Fleetnet America, clients have two options when calling for breakdown response or maintenance needs. The first is to have FleetNet locate a towing vendor for the customer to use. Once the job is complete, the vendor charges the customer directly. "In this case we do not have any say when it comes to the bill because we never see it," explains Nathan Jaynes, director of information technology for FleetNet. The second option — and the more popular by far — involves the customer asking FleetNet to take care of everything — setting up the job, following up with the vendor, and paying for the work. In this case, notes Jaynes, FleetNet audits the billing and pays the tow vendor directly.

In addition to coordinating heavy-duty towing for its members, says Carlson, "Insurance companies and claims adjusters turn to ATA to help mediate invoices following non-consensual recoveries — ensuring that invoices are fair and that recovery specialists are paid in a timely manner." Carlson notes that in addition to performing mediation on behalf of its trucking and insurance clients, ATA also works with its network towers when they are having a difficult time getting paid on a non-consensual recovery.

Located in South Bend, Ind., CDI Services, Inc., works with fleet maintenance providers who have 1,000 or more vehicles, as well as transportation fleets or companies that operate at least one truck.

According to Dana McFletcher, director of operations and sales, CDI's business units include emergency road service, fleet maintenance, a truck dealership, truck loading operations, truck driver training programs and employee payroll services.

CDI's client list consists of nearly 300 trucking, leasing, & fleet maintenance companies like Mayflower, Gilster Mary Lee Corporation, Frito Lay, United Van Lines and Highland Transport. When a truck breaks down, the driver calls CDI. The company then sets up a repair or towing job with one of its 60,000 contracted vendors. CDI handles nearly 5,000 customer calls each month, says McFletcher.

"We act as an extension to the customer's maintenance department in response to over-the-road emergencies and supply breakdown reports detailing the incident," explains McFletcher. When a customer or driver reports a breakdown, and CDI locates and sets up the vendor response, tracks the breakdown progress until the job is complete, and issues payment to the vendor when billing information is available. "Purchase order is our preferred method," says McFletcher, "however we are also capable of making comcheck and credit card payments." During the repair or towing operation, the company provides Internet access to real-time information and reports.

What are the advantages of joining a road service firm? According to Jaynes, "We're a single place you can call for a breakdown event, and we have vendor coverage in the U.S., Canada and Mexico." Jaynes points to fast response time as another plus when working with companies like FleetNet. "For the events that we did last year," he says, "our average time from receiving the call about a breakdown to the time that the vehicle was rolling again was just over two hours."

Jaynes also notes that the services provided by road service companies like FleetNet can be wide-ranging: "For some customers we handle 100 percent of their breakdown services," he says, "and for some we handle nights and weekends when their dispatchers are not available. We are very flexible in the services that we provide."

The billing debate

But the establishment of companies like ATA, CDI Services and FleetNet has caused a lot of grumbling in the towing community regarding the oversight of billing procedures — one of the services that the road service firms provide to their members. Earl Mumma of Highspire Auto & Truck Repair isn't necessarily a fan of the practice. "I feel they make a huge amount of money for a telephone call and then sometimes want to hassle the bill down," he explains.

"Personally I think they're doing more harm than good, but unfortunately so are some towers," says Bob Berry of Berry Brothers Towing in Oakland, Calif. Towers who do a substandard job can make the already heated situation even more difficult. "Unfortunately sometimes we give them all the ammo they need to do what they're doing and get sympathy from the public and from those who don't understand our industry," he explains.

While Berry agrees that there needs to be some mediation available in the industry, one problem with road service companies is that their mediators are not always fully knowledgeable about towing equipment or techniques, he says. "I've known a number of towers who have dealt with them on bills," explains Berry. "Sometimes they've delayed payments and run bills up for customers unnecessarily."

In addition, says Berry, not being on scene can lead to misunderstanding and incorrect information being used in the mediation process. "Unless they come out and take a look — unless they were there at a particular time, and were given the same instructions by the police department or the trucking company" — it can be difficult to negotiate a final bill, Berry explains.

For their part, the roadside service firms are concerned about protecting their members from being overcharged. "We've seen an increase in vendor rates nationwide," notes Dana McFletcher of CDI Services. "This in turn has caused an increase in customer complaints regarding costs being too high." One of the services that CDI provides for its members is to obtain estimates up front. "This is very helpful in avoiding or resolving disputes after the work is complete," explains McFletcher. To ensure that its customers are receiving "fair vendor pricing by passing through the cost as-is," she says, CDI bills its customer the actual vendor cost and taxes without invoice markups.

Nevertheless, some towers continue to view road service companies as a hindrance to getting the job done. "Big trucking companies and owners of fleets and organizations have set up these 'auto clubs' so they can run the price down on our work," says Berry.

Most of the time, says Berry, if a tower has set a fair, customary rate, he or she will receive very few complaints. "Unfortunately some towers double and triple their hourly rate unnecessarily," he says. Road service companies, adds Berry, sometimes fall into the same pattern: "They want to make 15, 20 or 25 percent off the job. They get paid right away." But the tower has to wait for payment. "Sometimes [road service companies] don't pay until 30, 60 or 90 days later," says Berry. The solution? Towers as well as road service companies need to make sure that rates are fair and that payment is immediate. "We can be our own worst enemy," Berry explains." If we want to solve our problems, we need to be as fair as possible."

Carlson notes that ATA is striving to work with towers to boost the industry's public image and the overall quality of work. "By and large the heavy towing industry is made up of solid business men and women who are working hard in dangerous conditions to keep our roadways moving," he says. "However, when we first came on the scene nine years ago, there were a number of towing companies that were utilizing abusive billing practices and were really hurting the image of the industry." To support its trucking clients and to improve the image of towers as a whole, says Carlson, ATA "aggressively battled companies that systematically preyed on the trucking industry."

Carlson admits that ATA's tough approach might have rubbed a number of towers the wrong way from time to time. But he adds that such disagreements are sometimes necessary in trying to negotiate the best possible deals for clients. "We took a lot of heat for this, but stayed the course because we knew that it was the right thing to do," explains Carlson. During the last several years ATA has moderated its approach and acts more as a mediator between towers and clients — both fleets and insurance companies — "to arrive at a bill that is fair," he says.

Making it better

When preparing a final bill, how can towers better assist their customers and, by extension, improve their relationships with road service companies? The solution involves more than just creating careful documentation of the incident response.

Also important, says Berry, is to establish a reasonable hourly rate. "Trucks come in different sizes, and may or may not be needed for a particular recovery job," he explains. Mumma agrees: "It is better to have an understanding of price before the job starts then there is no room for confusion," he says. "With technology today, on a recovery situation pictures of the recovery should be e-mailed to the company, and a rough estimate given before starting the job."

Towers should get paid as quickly as possible, says Mumma. Be careful to check out the companies prior to accepting a purchase order or accepting comcheck cards, he adds. "It is better to get paid when the job is done — before you leave the scene or tow job," he says. "Make sure your purchase order from any third-party vendor has an agreed amount," he says. Mumma knows some third parties like to call and negotiate the bill down after the job is done. "I would recommend all towers make all vendors sign a credit application so the customer understand their terms," adds Mumma. "With the economy today even big companies are trying to delay payments and this equates to interest-free loans for them."

If a truck arrives on scene but isn't specifically used for the recovery operation, it's important to take this into consideration when compiling a bill. "You need to come up with a figure for hand laborers who are, for example, unloading the trailer or helping with setting airbags," says Berry. "If those workers happen to drive up in a tow truck that isn't used at the scene, you don't need to charge for the truck. It was used as a mode of transportation — they could have arrived in an automobile instead," he says.

Berry notes that inexperience sometimes leads to billing issues. "Sometimes there are jobs that a tower hasn't done before," he explains, "and therefore things don't go as smoothly as if they had already done that job four or five times." When preparing a bill, adds Berry, people should take into account any learning curve "so the customer isn't impacted by somebody's inexperience."

The road service companies note that they carefully track their vendors' performance. "We do scrutinize the billing practices of our vendors," says Jaynes. "We hold them accountable for what they are charging for." In fact, says Jaynes, FleetNet cross-checks its vendors' rates and mileage against comparable towing firms to prevent price gouging.

To provide solid service to its members, ATA created a tower advisory group, or TAG, to assist with the company's policy and business decisions. "Our TAG group, consisting of 12 to 18 of what we believe to be the most solid companies in the nation, have been meeting with ATA staff on a regular basis," says Carlson. "The group helps us grow the business and ensure that we are doing everything that we can to improve the quality and image of heavy towing across the nation," he adds. ATA also works with highway oversight groups to ensure that they are considering the role of the heavy tower when developing policies for programs like quick clearance.

Empathy can go a long way toward resolving disagreements over a bill. Berry urges towers to look at the job from the customer's point of view: "Before you give a bill to the owner of a truck or car or bobtail — whatever you're working on — look at it from the other side," he says. "Ask yourself, 'Is this a fair bill for the work that was done?' Stand on the other side of the table and look at the bill. Would you think it's fair? If you think it is, then stick to your guns and collect the money you're owed."

The road service companies are well aware that their business rises and falls according to how they treat their customers. The companies build their networks of vendors by some of the same methods that local towers use to reach new customers. "We've built up over time using OEM listings, truck stops, referrals and the like," explains McFletcher. The quality of CDI's vendors is tracked using a rating system based on service, price, response time and billing practices.

"With truck freight dropping by record levels of 35 to 40 percent," says Carlson, "our company doubled our sales staff to attract more fleets to use our services." Additionally, he says, ATA is working on strategic partnerships designed to bring more tow volume to its network while better serving the company's trucking clients.

Attitude and future plans

Towers and road service companies agree that attitude is paramount in negotiating a final bill. "You have to be very sure that you're doing the right thing and charging the right rate," says Berry. "Otherwise it will come across when you're talking to people, and you won't project what you need to in order to support that bill." Sometimes tow truck drivers can be defensive, says Berry — which can work against them when dealing with an insurance company, a road service firm, "or the guy standing on the other side of the desk, trying to get his car back."

Whether or not towers are happy with the growth of the road service companies, says Earl Mumma, it's something that is growing and changing the traditional way of doing business. "This is a change the towing industry has to adapt to," he says.

"I would like to think that we have done an effective job in connecting the best trucking companies with the best towers," says Chris Carlson of ATA. "I do believe that with our active participation in both trucking and towing associations that we have helped to bridge the gap between the two industries. I also believe that because of our relationships with trucking associations and highway commissions that we are impacting how our roadways will be quickly and safely cleared in the future," he explains.

"I've been doing this 36 years," says Bob Berry. "You learn to do the job a little bit better every day. You *need* to do things better every day, and try to be as fair as possible." Berry reiterates his "golden rule" about billing: try to see things from the customer's point of view. "Do unto others as you would have them do unto you," says Berry. "It's an old rule, but it works."

Regardless of how towers view their billing practices and the role of the new road service companies, Carlson urges everyone to work together to find the best ways to bill their customers. "I'd like to encourage those reading this article to continue to fight the good fight in the midst of one of the most difficult economic times in recent history," he says.

Documenting the job

If you're concerned about someone getting a negative impression of your billing practices, you can protect yourself to a great extent by making sure that your documentation is complete, clear and concise. "It's all in the writeup of the incident," says Kevin Farthing, owner of Waffco Heavy Duty Towing & Recovery in Lake Station, Ind.

To help with their paperwork, Farthing and his staff use a software package called Tracker Enterprise, produced by Tracker Management Systems of Cleveland, Ohio. The company works with towing firms to improve their dispatch capability, impound and storage lot management, GPS tracking of vehicle fleets, and office automation needs. For preparing solid documentation, the Tracker Enterprise software "has awesome note boxes and also a great itemization page for billing," notes Farthing.

In addition to using computer-based tracking systems, Farthing has a few tips for his fellow towers that will make the invoicing process — and any disagreements that arise from it — resolve much more smoothly:

Document what happened — immediately following the job.

"When we come back from an incident, regardless of the size, the person who supervised the job sits down and writes a rather lengthy note of the scenario," explains Farthing. This information includes what the team found upon arrival, what type of equipment was used on the job, how much damage was done to the vehicle or vehicles involved in the incident, and the tower's general opinion of the crash — speed on a curve, snow or ice on the road, and other key issues.

Use decimal places in your numbers.

Farthing avoids rounding any numbers in his invoices. "For example, if I charge $150.00 per hour for a piece of equipment and I use it for 1.06 hours, the total charge will be $159.00," says Farthing. "I don't round the hour up or down." Farthing has seen some invoices from other companies that do round the dollar amount. "This always looks to me to be pulled from thin air," he says. The Tracker computer software allows all times to be documented, adds Farthing, "since you are rarely out working an even number of hours." For example, if Farthing starts a job at 8:11 and finishes at 9:33, he enters those exact times into the software program rather than rounding the job to something like 90 minutes.

Be as precise as possible.

To avoid long arguments over why you billed for a particular service, carefully write down exactly what you accomplished, says Farthing. "If the average tow operator would look at his paperwork like he does when he gets an itemization invoice from the dealership for repairs to his truck, he would do better with his invoicing," he says.

The still or video camera has proven to be a powerful tool for documenting what occurred at an accident scene. Farthing highly recommends that towers take photos and video whenever possible.

Start taking photos when you arrive on scene.

"Always have first-arrival pictures, and have a time and date stamp on the photos," says Farthing. "This helps to back up the invoicing." Farthing recommends that towers walk back up the road "and get a long shot of the road, ramp, ditch — whatever was the precursor to the accident." If cargo was involved, says Farthing, take lots of photographs to document the scene.

Video can be helpful as well.

You don't have to use an expensive video camera — just one that can help you obtain clear visual evidence of what happened during the recovery job. "We video some jobs during the hardest or longest part of the recovery," explains Farthing, "to show the amount of labor, equipment, conditions and where the equipment went."

Finally, remember that it's all in the approach. "As they say, attitude determines altitude," says Farthing. "I've heard more than one tow operator tell a customer, 'That's the price, and if you don't like it, I'll see you in court!' Well, you know what? Some companies have teams of lawyers and insurance companies that will make you regret your bravado and attitude."

If a customer questions you, says Farthing, don't take offense. "They're just like us," he explains. "They're trying to justify the bills." See if there's something you can do to improve the transaction. Farthing sometimes slashes a few days off storage fees, lets the customer comcheck him for payment, or allows the customer to come in at his or her leisure to move out any salvage items. "Try to make a new customer, not a new enemy," urges Farthing.

A Hard Fight:
New Jersey, Private Property Towing,
and State Regulation

Several years ago, towers in New Jersey were involved in a battle with the state legislature over a scourge to towing companies and vehicle owners alike: predatory towers.

"It was a hard fight," said John Glass, president of the Garden State Towman's Association and owner of Morristown Auto Body, Inc., in Morristown, N.J. Looking back, Glass marvels at how the issue rapidly exploded over the course of several months. "It started with legislation for private property towing, then turned into this major thing with the insurance industry, the attorney general, the state division of consumer affairs — all of these people involved."

189

Round One

Though predatory towers had been a problem for the industry for many years, public outrage pushed the issue to the forefront. In New Jersey, horror stories about predators abounded, and the media took the towing industry to task in newspapers, television, over the radio and on the Internet.

In 2006, extensive coverage in the Bergen County newspaper *The Record* blew the lid off the issue, and the state legislature got involved. Assemblyman Robert Gordon co-sponsored a bill called The Predatory Towing Prevention Act. "While parking rules and regulations are absolutely necessary to help keep order on our roadways," Gordon said at the time, "dishonest towing companies will not be permitted to make their money by patrolling parking lots without permission, and charging excessive rates to release impounded vehicles. This law will ensure that property owners have the final say over vehicles that are parked, legally and illegally, on their property."

In October 2007, New Jersey Governor Jon Corzine signed the Predatory Towing Prevention Act into law. The new regulations dealt strictly with private trespassing and how and when towing companies, under contract, could pull vehicles from privately owned areas. But a simple yet powerful phrase in the legislation — *nonconsensual towing* — triggered a huge dustup between towers and a fairly new opponent: the insurance industry.

According to Glass, the insurance industry wanted to establish a flat fee for nonconsensual towing. "They don't like the idea that every tow bill is different," said Glass. "It's not consistent. There's winching involved, there's cleanup involved; in some parts of the state the bill is lower, in some parts higher. [The insurers] wanted more control over the rates by having the state of New Jersey set those rates."

Ironically, New Jersey towers supported the Predatory Towing Prevention Act in its original form as a simple way to handle a rapidly worsening problem. But once the insurance industry stepped in, "it blew up because legislators didn't understand what we do," said Glass. "All they hear is a lot of complaints."

Like the towers, the insurance companies were trying to protect their business interests: "The objective of the insurance companies is to contain costs, and to drop prices," explained Glass. To that end, representatives for the insurance industry made their case in front of the state legislature — a case that, Glass said, painted a picture that wasn't always accurate. "After they made their speech," recalled Glass, "we had to stand up and say, 'I beg to differ.'"

In making their argument, the New Jersey towers tried to be equitable. "We had to admit there was some abuse," said Glass. "But we also had to prove that the data the insurance industry was showing to the state wasn't always on the up and up." Among other things, continued Glass, the insurers inflated their figures to make it sound like towers were charging too much. One method of accomplishing this was to include towing and storage in a lump sum, said Glass. By doing the math this way, insurers could quote figures at, for example, $700 for a single tow.

One of the difficulties in settling the issues surrounding the bill was the extensive media coverage that dominated the airwaves, Internet and print for months on end. "Every time we turned around," recalled Glass, "there was another horror story on TV and in the newspaper. This wasn't anything new, though. But the more you report it, the more people come out of the woodwork, and it builds. Then the legislation builds up so much steam it gets out of control."

According to Glass, GSTA's efforts to mount a clear, truthful campaign proved highly effective. If a tower was ever challenged by a legislator or a newspaper reporter, said Glass, "we could explain things to them — and back up what we were saying. Whereas, the insurance industry, with all their knowledge, couldn't do it."

Round Two

But the new law wasn't quite the legislation that New Jersey towers had hoped for, so they supported an amendment that would curtail some of the requirements of the law while clarifying other areas. GSTA met with the New Jersey Division of Consumer Affairs and representatives from the insurance industry. The results of those meetings were positive. "We were able to draft definitions and a list of items that the state of

New Jersey recognized as chargeable work for nonconsensual tows," said Glass.

Glass urged New Jersey towers to support the amendment. "This law in its current state will devastate the New Jersey towing industry," wrote Glass. "Its effect is far reaching into every aspect of our business including private contracts and public contracts with municipalities and toll roads." Glass noted that the amendment would bring [the law] back to its original intent of controlling *only* private property towing." On January 9, 2010, the revised legislation was signed into law.

The revised state law, which clarified what towers could invoice as chargeable items, was a fresh approach to a long-term problem. The law also reworked the relationship between municipalities and the towing companies that operate within local boundaries.

Prior to the new state law, local ordinances often crippled towers by establishing flat rates that didn't always mesh with the amount of work required. "A town could say, for example, cleanup and administrative fees, and maybe some labor, should be included in the basic towing fee," said Glass. "They wouldn't allow towers to charge any additional fees, even if they were for extra steps to complete a job."

Now, however, towers can go to their town councils and argue their case by pointing to the new state law. The "menu" of chargeable items is very clearly spelled out. "Now you can say to the municipality, 'These *are* extra steps, and should be additional chargeable items, because the *state* recognizes them as such," said Glass.

Any disputes are also settled on the local level. "If there's a complaint, you deal with it on your home turf," explained Glass. If the problem can't be resolved within the city limits, it can be kicked upstairs to the state division of consumer affairs.

One of the other big issues discussed, said Glass, was the use of administrative fees in billing. The insurance industry felt that administrative fees shouldn't be a separately billable item and was "just a part of doing business." Here again, GSTA worked hard to explain the topic to the state legislators. "We gave them a definition of it, showed them what was involved," recalled Glass. "They understood. They came back and said, 'We feel that's a billable item.'"

The next battle?

So far, so good — but that doesn't mean towers can rest easy, said Glass, who predicts that the insurance industry will try again soon. "I'm sure we're going to see another legislative bill show up in the future when the timing is right." The recent tussle over the Predatory Towing Prevention Act was the third time in the last 10 to 15 years that Glass has seen insurers attempt to control the billing practices of the towing industry through legislation.

Glass feels that insurers are scrutinizing the towing industry more today than ever. "The insurance companies have a lot of power, a lot of clout, a lot of lobbyists," said Glass. "They have the ability to affect legislation in good and bad ways, and they're not worried about the survival of the towing industry. They just want it to get done the cheapest way possible."

And, Glass warns, "it's not happening only in New Jersey. Like I said, insurance companies are looking for every possible way to contain costs. That's their job." Glass has noticed that other states are looking at how towing companies invoice customers for tows that fall under the auspices of the insurance companies.

Glass likens the insurance companies' efforts to those of motor clubs in the recent past. Both industries attempted to control costs by choosing their own, low-cost, towing companies. "Motor clubs came in and reshaped the towing industry by taking a lot of work out of the private sector," he explained. Although the motor clubs were able to centralize towing services in many areas by essentially controlling dispatch operations for their members, "in the long run, this has kind of failed," said Glass. "They have the work, but they have more and more trouble finding towers who are willing to do it, and do it well."

Why? Like the insurance companies, the motor clubs tried to slice costs where they could, only to undercut their own effectiveness, said Glass. For towers, working as subordinates to motor clubs is often bad for the bottom line. "There's just not a lot of money in it," explained Glass.

Strength in numbers

Glass compliments the members of the Garden State Towman's Association who helped effect changes to the Predatory Towing Prevention Act. "Lots of GSTA people worked on it," said Glass. "They made every meeting and contributed a tremendous amount of their time." Glass specifically wanted to thank Joe Haines and Rick Malanga, two of the organization's vice presidents. "They were beside me all the way through," said Glass.

The GSTA's recent victory over the insurance companies in New Jersey, noted Glass, is a good example of how towers, working together, can protect their businesses from being overrun with regulations that can damage the quality of the work. "This is the advantage of having a strong association," said Glass. "We are successful in our legislation because we go in and ask for things that make sense — things that need to be done."

And they do it, added Glass, without the use of lobbyists or high-powered attorneys. "We do it ourselves. We go in with our heads held high, and give truthful and accurate information." This straightforward approach, explained Glass, made all the difference in the recent battle over New Jersey's towing legislation. "It worked out well for our industry," said Glass.

Tracking the Trucks:
Automatic Vehicle Location Systems

A dispatcher peers at a computer monitor, watching colorful graphics move across a map of the local area. Icons representing tow trucks shift positions on the screen. At a glance, the dispatcher knows exactly where all of the company's vehicles are located on the road — and how well the drivers are doing their jobs.

Having the capability to track and move a vehicle fleet in this fashion is an increasingly popular option for towing companies nationwide. In Austin, Texas, Ronny New of Southside Wrecker, Inc., received a call about a vehicle that was washed into a river. One of New's tow trucks was dispatched to the vehicle's last known location, but nobody could find the missing vehicle.

New checked out his Networkfleet GPS system. The computer showed New the terrain via satellite maps, which let him pinpoint the

195

area in the river where the vehicle was located. Using the GPS tracking system, New could see the missing vehicle's location on his computer map and was able to direct the tow truck toward the vehicle.

This is only one example of the usefulness of a fleet-wide Automatic Vehicle Location (AVL) system, powered by GPS technology, that gives towing companies unprecedented ability to manage their vehicle fleets. In turn, towers can provide faster, more helpful service to their customers.

System types

The increasing use of GPS navigation systems in passenger vehicles is no surprise, and neither is the increasing use of AVL systems at today's towing companies. Companies like Telenav, Vericom Technologies, and Transportation Information Systems provide hardware/software combinations and technical support that help towing companies oversee their fleets more efficiently.

AVL is also used by government agencies like the Bay Area Freeway Service Patrol, which contracts for private tow trucks to take care of approximately 550 miles of freeway in the San Francisco area. The project is operated jointly by the Metropolitan Transportation Commission Service Authority for Freeways and Expressways, the California Highway Patrol and the California Department of Transportation. Part of the system's $2 million worth of communications equipment is dedicated to an AVL system that watches the locations of the 83 tow trucks assigned to the Freeway Service Patrol.

The ability to track a fleet of vehicles requires technology that can range from simple to sophisticated, depending on the needs of the company running an AVL system. While almost all of these systems utilize satellites, the most extensivesystems make use of two-way satellite technology to track their targets. "An example of this would be Qualcomm — many large truck fleet companies use this," says Jim Weaver, chairman and CEO of Tracker Management Systems, Inc., in Cleveland, Ohio.

Qualcomm's technology helps truck dispatchers keep watch over their fleets. "The advantage is 100-percent coverage with communication anywhere in the United States." However, says Weaver, the system's disadvantage is its cost: "It's too expensive to justify usage across the board in the towing industry."

The more widely used solutions piggyback on existing phone services such as Nextel, Verizon and AT&T, says Weaver. By utilizing the data package of the cell phone carrier they're already using, towing companies can track their vehicles while keeping costs low. "The software utilizes the telephone's data plan to send information back and forth to the office computer/dispatch and mapping screen," explains Weaver. With this type of service, he adds, a towing company can get basic GPS for as little as an additional $10.00 per month. Adding custom software on the phone will greatly enhance the benefits while still keeping the cost very low.

A third option involves installing Mobile Data Terminals (MDTs) in each vehicle. MDTs provide two-way communications between drivers and their home offices. "This type of solution offers the ability to monitor and or control functions in the vehicle," says Weaver. MDTs allow towing companies to monitor a tow truck's PTO activity, disengage the starter, lock and unlock doors, track whether the light beacons are in use, and monitor driver activity like speed, quick stops and quick turns.

Data can be displayed inside the cab of the tow truck, allowing the driver to respond immediately. "With all information including the option of driving directions," says Weaver, "the driver can then complete the call without the need to talk with dispatch."

San Diego-based Networkfleet, Inc., is one of the companies that provide this type of system. "Networkfleet combines frequent GPS location tracking with precise diagnostic monitoring to give fleets a complete and accurate picture of their vehicle operations," says Craig Whitney, vice president of marketing. By connecting directly to a vehicle's onboard computer, Networkfleet collects information such as vehicle speed, diagnostic trouble codes and miles per gallon. Fleet managers log in to a secure web site to view location and diagnostics data. Fleet managers can also receive instant e-mail notifications when exceptions occur or pre-set thresholds are exceeded.

Big benefits

Towers have put the features of AVL systems to good use. Bruce Pedigo, vice president of operationsfor Joe's Towing & Recovery in Bloomington, Ill., uses the FleetMatics and BudgetGPS systems at his company. Pedigo's fleet is varied: he operates five heavy-duty tow trucks, 14 light-duty trucks and flatbeds, four semi tractors and three road service units. The FleetMatics system consists of a GPS box mounted underneath the dashboard of the vehicle, while BudgetGPS uses a cell phone mounted in a lockbox behind the seat of the truck. Pedigo is gradually converting his fleet to BudgetGPS, primarily as a cost-cutting measure.

"Calls and trucks are mapped on the same computer screen," explains Pedigo. "This allows the dispatchers to dispatch the driver closest to the call, and quote appropriate ETAs by seeing the drop location on a map in comparison to the call they are taking."

"All dispatch stations have dual monitors for their computers," continues Pedigo. "The GPS runs on one monitor so there is no switching between their towing software and the GPS. BudgetGPS also integrates with our towing software (the TOPS dispatch management system from TowXchange), so that calls are mapped on the same screen as the GPS."

Earl Mumma, owner of Highspire Auto & Truck Repair in Steelton, Penn., has 20 wreckers, service trucks, carriers and miscellaneous vehicles in his fleet. Mumma purchased his AVL system from Teletrac, Inc., of Garden Grove, Calif. "It's for the convenience of the customers, and for me to be able to tell when trucks are in a certain area," he explains. The Teletrac unit in each truck is not visible to the operator — it's hidden inside the dashboard. Among its other features, Mumma's AVL system allows his dispatchers to monitor the location and speed of each truck, "full tracking and reporting turn-by-turn, and printable reports."

In Woodstock, Ga., Mike Patellis, a 31-year veteran of the industry, has had as many as 51 trucks in his inventory at Alpha Towing, depending on the nature of the business during a particular year. Patellis installed the i-Trac GPS system in 12 of his trucks. "We love it, and the drivers love it," says Patellis. "It helps our drivers if they get lost. It helps us give the customer an accurate ETA without having to bother the driver as he's on his way."

The system is also highly flexible: "We can dispatch from anywhere, anytime — at the shop, at home, even at the beach," says Patellis. System updates aren't quite in real-time, but they're close: Patellis says that the i-Trac in his office updates every nine seconds.

Critical in any AVL setup, says Patellis, is the quality of the person who's operating the system in the shop. "You need a good dispatcher," he says. "Someone who will use the tools that the GPS system offers." A knowledgeable dispatcher can use AVL technology to re-route trucks as needed and provide accurate ETAs to pending rush calls, thereby providing better coverage, fuel burn and time, says Patellis.

Maintenance, safety and peace of mind

Onboard systems like these are also useful in announcing when vehicles are due for routine maintenance. "It tells us when the truck is due for an oil change or tire rotation," says Patellis. "It's a great monitor of the fleet, with great reports you would never think about — demographics of your accounts, service area, volume, miles to site, towed, waiting time, and time out of service."

Patellis also notes that the reports generated by his AVL system prove to the local government — the Department of Transportation, for example — that his trucks are being maintained properly and driven within DOT limits.

"We use the system to track our trucks' locations for dispatch efficiency as well as to keep an eye on our trucks to see how they're being driven," says Charles White, manager of Retriever Towing in Portland, Ore. Retriever Towing operates a 10-truck fleet performing private-property towing in the Portland metropolitan area.

White's company purchased its system from BudgetGPS about four years ago. The system consists of a Nextel phone equipped only with a data plan. The phone is hardwired to a charger inside the truck. Data from the phone is accessed via computers in Retriever Towing's main office. "Our managers use the system to track complaints and as evidence of complaints or misuse of our trucks," explains White.

Another benefit of certain AVL systems is the ability to track towing operations remotely: "Any computer can click on and watch us," says Patellis. "We can give you a special code to log in with." This is a helpful option for clients who are anxious about how their vehicles are being treated: "It's good for the customer with the $250,000 car," explains Patellis.

If a truck temporarily moves out of range — through tunnels, mountainous areas or low terrain, for example — Patellis notes that the AVL system keeps data in its memory and reports it to the office whenever the truck reconnects with the system.

Printable reports are a big help, says Mumma. "If there ever was a collision, we have proof of vehicle speed." Adds Pedigo: "If questions arise as to what driver handled a call, [or] we receive a complaint about where a driver was located or the speed he was running, we pull the data for that time frame to deny or confirm the complaint."

Patellis put this into action when one of his tow trucks was recently involved in an accident. The State Patrol cited the driver for speeding. Patellis had his AVL system kick out a history of the truck's movements. Then he burned the information onto a CD and handed it to the State Patrol. The computer data showed speed, time and directions — and clearly demonstrated that the tow truck driver was driving under the speed limit.

Helping the drivers

An AVL system is also useful for company owners who need to keep an eye on any drivers who might be performing below the company's standards. According to Patellis, his system has helped to drop internal theft to almost zero. In addition, "It sends e-mails to the boss if the truck is over the limit for things like time, speed, and location," he says.

For those drivers who might take their eye off the ball, Mumma notes that the system encourages drivers to stay alert on the job. "It keeps your drivers focused on work, not personal issues or side trips, things like that," explains Mumma.

For drivers who are unsure about the local geography, AVL systems can help navigate tow trucks to their destinations. "We've used it many times to help drivers get to a breakdown location in areas that they are not familiar with," says Pedigo. "The system helps the dispatcher know if the driver has gone too far or not far enough, and direct the driver to where he needs to be."

Sometimes the tracking capability comes in handy during rather unusual situations. When one of Patellis' trucks went into the dealership for a repair, the mechanic decided to take the truck for a 100-mile tow for his father. "Oops!" says Patellis. "The GPS told on him." In the end, Patellis charged the mechanic for the tow — and got his truck repaired for free.

What would you add?

AVL truck-mounted systems differ greatly in features and cost, explains Weaver, withthe very basic unit costing $300 and about $20 a month per truck to as high as $4,000 or more per unit and over $400 per month per truck. "So someone who wants to automate their fleet should really consider what exact features they want and the budget they have to do it," says Weaver. "In the end, talking with companies that offer more than one product,and determining whatfeatures you want,will help an owner get the closest match to his expectations and budget."

Cost aside, towers have ideas about what they'd like to add to their AVL systems. White, for example, would love to have true real-time tracking and onboard video capability.

Pedigo would like to use one GPS unit to report the location tracking info to the dispatchers, plus enable the driver to use the unit as a "Tom Tom"— a navigation system similar to those installed in passenger cars. "Both dispatchers and drivers would be seeing the same information which would reduce the amount of equipment needed in the truck," says Pedigo. "We would make it so that one system both maps the calls on the same screen that trucks are showing on and has the reporting such as PTO, engine, mileage, et cetera."

Automatic Vehicle Location is just one more example of how technology is changing — and, in many cases, improving — the way towers do business. Patellis points to how the AVL system boosts his bottom line. "If you have a service vehicle of any type," he says, "you are not as smart as I am if you don't have a GPS system. In a sense, I 'own the road' because I can access GPS service reports."

Moreover, Patellis does a brisk business with just five trucks in a highly competitive area. When asked how he succeeds, he points to the capabilities of his AVL system and answers, "The one with the most knowledge wins!"

The Art of Selling Parts

It's a Saturday evening in the small town of New Hampton, Iowa. At Zip's Truck Equipment, parts manager Todd Suhr is getting ready to head home when his phone rings. He picks up the receiver. On the other end of the line is a tow truck operator from Spearfish, South Dakota — nearly 700 miles to the west. The tower is trapped in a furious ice storm, and his truck just sputtered to a halt. He checked under the hood and realized that his power take-off (PTO) is broken. He needs the part, and he needs it now.

"No problem," Suhr tells the frustrated tower. Suhr grabs a PTO off the shelf and jumps in his car. His wife gets in the passenger seat, and the couple drives as fast as they can, crossing the border into South Dakota and motoring across the state to meet the tower at a halfway point. It's 3 a.m. when Suhr hands the part to the grateful tower, who installs the new PTO and gets back to work in the ice storm. Suhr and his wife turn around and head back to Iowa — a 350-mile trip.

There's no doubt that towers and the businesses that support them are dedicated people. But personally driving nine hours to deliver a part, in an ice storm no less? "I don't do that very often," admits Suhr. But he knew that the tow truck had to get back in service quickly, and so he took care of the problem, no questions asked.

Parts experts like Todd Suhr go the extra mile to support their customers — and keep the tow trucks on the road so that the drivers can support *their* customers.

What they carry

Parts vendors are located all across the country. Nick Kemper runs TowPartsNow.com, a supplier in Portland, Ore., that takes orders via the telephone and over the Internet. What types of tow truck parts does the company stock? Just about anything you can name, says Kemper. "Wheel lift straps and lockout tools are the most commonly purchased items," he adds. "Other big sellers are carrier skates, dollies,carrier winch cables, two-inch ratchets and magnetic tow lights."

In Shullsburg, Wisc., shop foreman Mark Pollock handles emergency parts orders, among his many duties. Pollock works for Truck Country, which has 12 truck dealerships in Wisconsin and Iowa. He says that the company's extensive inventory features recovery straps, chains, V-bridles, minor service kits for valves, and dollies. Truck Country's shop stock primarily includes general repair items — "parts that move quickly," explains Pollock. This also includes cables, chains, and lights.

Brand dealerships obviously carry their sponsors' products but also stock a variety of parts for other types of vehicles. Zip's Truck Equipment carries parts for all major brands but focuses on Miller Industries trucks since they're an official distributor for Miller. "We stock parts for every major brand, and of course accessories," says Suhr.

What types of parts sell the most? "Wheel lift and carrier straps and winch cable are going to wear out naturally and need to be replaced often," says Kemper. "Latch kits for safety hooks — both on the end of winch cables and safety chains — replace the original latch, so that the hook retains its safety features." At Zip's, Suhr notes that he sells a lot of parts that are replacements for parts that have worn out: wear pads, pivot pin kits and bushings, to name a few.

"The majority of parts we sell as *supposed* to wear out," says John LaMarche, president of Crawford Truck Sales in Lancaster, Mass. This includes parts like slide-back kits for rollbacks, winch cables and accessories. "We also sell a lot of grids and L-arms that are lost due to driver error or sometimes from being stolen," adds LaMarche.

If a part isn't readily available, LaMarche keeps five to 10 kits in stock that he and his staff can disassemble to retrieve specific parts. "This usually happens for parts that aren't wear-out pieces or aren't a common item," explains LaMarche, or when a truck is involved in a collision and needs a specific part.

Handling customer orders

Customers dial in from all over the nation and from overseas as well. Truck Country is based in Wisconsin, but Pollock hears from towers in Michigan, Connecticut, the Carolinas and Wyoming, to name a few.

Competition among parts sellers is heating up, says Butch Hogland, owner of Hooks Towing & Recovery Supplies in Wynne, Ark. "Some of the biggest challenges that we face today are supplying the product with a great price, and also with a great product to match," he says. "There's a lot of competition out there — tons more than there used to be. "You have 'price buyers' and then you have 'product buyers,' so you have to be able to keep up with the market on pricing and product to keep all the buyers happy."

Vendors use a variety of selling methods to attract customers. Kevin Hamman launched his own business, Hamman Engineering, in 1991 after towers and distributors contacted him looking for parts after the local Holmes plant in Newbern, Tenn., closed. "I started out supplying Holmes parts," explains Hamman. "I soon began receiving requests for chains, cables and other accessories. The demand grew until I found myself selling parts and accessories full-time."

Hamman recently launched an eBay store to see if it would boost sales. The results have been mixed. "It has helped somewhat but the profit margins make it hardly worth messing with," he says. "First of all, eBay's closing value fees start at 8 percent. Then, PayPal charges around 3 percent to handle the transaction." Add to that the fact that margins are low due to stiff competition in the marketplace, "and you can see why it is difficult to make money on eBay," says Hamman.

When customers phone in a parts order, sometimes they request a specific part, and sometimes they need assistance to troubleshoot the problem they're having. "Often they don›t know exactly what they need, or what they have," says Kemper. "Sometimes a lot of research is required, and a lot of interaction with the parts representatives at the major manufacturers." Over the years Kemper has grown relationships with a network of industry sources that he taps for help when he needs it. "I send out a blanket e-mail to all of them and see who gets back to me first," says Kemper. "They get rather competitive!"

Kemper enjoys doing research and "digging around to find something out-of-the-ordinary for a customer," he says, "because you learn from that and help that customer, who is usually very grateful for the extra effort."

Pinpointing the required part takes knowledge and patience on the part of the parts seller. "A lot of times they know what's wrong but they don't know why," says Pollock, who then guides the customer through a diagnosis over the phone. "I ask certain questions," he says. "What is it doing? When the customer starts leading me toward a certain issue, I can pinpoint it for them a little better."

If a customer has an idea of what he or she needs, Pollock says they can go to Truck Country's Web site, which contains online versions of parts catalogs and service manuals. "A lot of the calls I get are towers who kind of know what they're looking for but aren't sure where to find it," adds Mark. Parts breakdowns are also available online at Zip's Web site.

Most sales are still done over the telephone, says LaMarche of Crawford Truck Sales. "We start by getting the most important details: their model and serial number and brand of chassis," he explains. "Even though we're a Jerr-Dan dealer, we do sell all brands of parts. Then we try to walk the customer through to get the right generation of part they need."

"We also have some items on eBay," adds LaMarche. "We're trying a lot of different avenues to get parts to the customer." Even with Internet sales growing, LaMarche notes that most of his customers prefer to order by phone, even if they first locate the part they need on the Internet.

Like many other parts stores, Crawford Truck Sales takes Internet orders 24 hours a day. At Zip's Truck Equipment, Suhr notes that the company is doing an increasing amount of business — about 10 percent — over the Internet via the company's online e-store.

"Online ordering is a big advantage for customerswho workshifts that don't allow them to call during the core business hours," says Bruce Bahman, marketing manager for AW Direct.Bahman adds that the company's Web site allows AW Direct to connect with customers that the company might not be able to reach with a catalog, or customers who just prefer to order online. "In my opinion," says Bahman, "there aren't any disadvantages as long aswe providecomplete, up-to-dateinformationto the customer and continually addrelevant newcontent."

AW Direct currently ships its products directly from warehouses in Wisconsin and Connecticut. Bahman adds that the company is working on a distribution upgrade for 2010 that will allow products to ship fromfour regional warehouses to reach almost all customers in the U.S. in one to two business days.

Getting the parts to the customer

Sometimes parts managers hear from customers who need a part immediately. At Truck Country, Pollock got a call late on a Friday afternoon from a tower in northern Michigan. "There was nobody around him, and everyone around him had already closed," recalls Pollock. "He was all alone." The tower had blown a pump on his Ford wrecker. "He thought he had a bad valve, but after running him through some checks he found out that he had a bad pump," says Pollock.

Pollock checked his computer parts database and spent the next 45 minutes on the phone with the tower and several parts suppliers until he located the right pump. "We were able to overnight it to him so he could get back on the road," says Pollock.

At Zip's Truck Equipment, Suhr estimates that one out of every 15 orders is from a customer who needs the part immediately. But in reality, he says, all parts orders are critical. "Most of the orders are for a truck that's down," says Suhr. "It makes a lot of the orders urgent in their own way." Suhr and his staff pride themselves on quick response time: by helping repair tow trucks, "we keep the drivers working so they're making money," he explains.

Ninety-nine percent of the orders coming out of Zip's are shipped via UPS. Suhr appreciates the delivery service's ability to track packages as they travel to the customer. "It's really easy to find out where the part is, from the time it leaves here to the time it gets there. I have a tracking number, so I can check online to tell the customer exactly where the package is at any time."

"If customers need something right away, we can meet them here at the shop or find a way to get it to them," says Suhr, who's been working parts for 15 years. "We have well over a million dollars in parts and accessories on hand, so we have more direct control and don't have to rely on others. "Nowadays with people using credit cards, we can ship parts directly from the supplier to the customer. We only ship direct when absolutely necessary." This saves on time and freight costs.

Change of season, change of parts

At Truck Country, the parts that sell the most depend on what time of year it is. During the fall, says Pollock, "a lot of towers are looking at their wreckers, checking their cables, their chains, lights, that kind of thing." When that happens, Pollock sells a lot of service kits — items such as oil filters, hydraulic filters, and seal valve replacements.

Different types of parts begin to move in the springtime. "At that time of the year we usually sell a lot of carrier items, 50-foot wire ropes, V-bridles and the occasional light bar," says Pollock.

Another item known to wear out is hoses. "I think everybody had gone to using a cheaper hose," says Pollock. "So the hoses just don't last like they used to. Some towers I've talked to have changed three or four hoses on one wrecker in a 12-month period." On older tow trucks, Pollock says he's heard from towers who have almost never changed hoses.

However, Pollock also notes that the vendors are hearing the complaints and are making efforts to upgrade the quality of their products. "I don't know whether vendors were getting bad materials or what, but that's turned around now," he says. The frequency of replacing bad hoses in the first few years of operation is declining due to the use of better quality products during manufacturing, adds Pollock.

Improvements and innovations

As parts sellers, people like Nick Kemper are careful to verify that what they stock is of good quality. "There are always new things to look at, and innovations being made," says Kemper. "A lot of times things sound good, and you make an attempt to market them, but there isn't much interest." Just because something sounds or looks good doesn't mean it will sell, says Kemper. "Making the tried-and-true stuff last longer and more safe is what the customer really wants."

Over the years, Suhr has seen major improvements in safety gear and apparel, including rated chains and straps that are made for specific uses or needs. He's also seen major improvements in driver training materials and training opportunities.

Parts sellers also do their best to protect the customer. "If it isn't safe, we won't sell it," says Kemper. "For example, we will not sell Grade 40 chain and hooks, because really, for the type of work our customers are doing, Grade 70 is the minimum strength they should be using."

Pollock notes that manufacturers are constantly working to improve the seals on pumps and winches to increase the lifespan of each product. In addition, Pollock sees technological advances in the tow trucks he sells and repairs: "They're putting more up-to-date electronics in these wreckers — multiplexing control stations, emergency shut-downs, the ability to send data back to your home base with wi-fi networks, and full-function wireless remote control of wrecker functions." The use of wireless remote control is a good safety idea, says Pollock, because it keeps the operator out of harm's way and gives him better sight of the recovery that he is performing.

For Suhr, the use of LED lighting has been one of the best improvements of the last 10 or 15 years. "Of course the price has gone up," says Suhr, "but using LEDs helps make other things on the truck work better because the LEDs don't use as much power." Overall, says Suhr, the LEDs are less of a load on a truck's electrical systems.

"Many of the design improvements in the products we sellrelate to ease of use by the operator in towing and recovery," says Hamman. Examples include the popularity of heavy-duty rotators, the widespread use of hydraulic self-loading wheel lifts, and fifth-wheel underlifts that can go on and off a chassis in minutes. "We have seen a shift toward lighter-weight materials for equipment that is handled by the operator," adds Hamman. "An example would be the Collins Ultralight Dolly that not only has aluminum axles but aluminum hubs as well."

Kemper agrees: "The Collins ultra-lightweight self-loading dolly is probably the best innovation I've seen in the last few years," he says.He points to the product's decrease in weight and simultaneous increase in strength as a combination that is "tough to beat."Kemper's opinion is born of experience: "As someone who drove a tow truck for 15 years, and who lifted those dollies many thousands of times, dropping a significant amount of weight is a tangible benefit," he says."Now they've come out with some sharp-looking aluminum wheels for their dollies, and we're seeing another surge in sales."

Behind the parts desk, the computerization of the supply inventory has proven helpful time and time again when a customer dials in a parts order. "Our database keeps track of the inventory," says Suhr. "At the same time, we can track customers' records, including everything the customer has bought since day one." This is useful when tracking individual customer's requirements and parts needed for a specific tow truck. "I can go clear back to 1991 and look at what they bought way back then," notes Suhr.

So next time your tow truck needs some tender loving care, know that the parts experts are ready to do whatever it takes to get your vehicle back in running order. "Overall I think the products being made now are doing a better of making the tow operator's job a little easier and safer," says Pollock. "The towing industry as a whole is starting to keep up better, to make the job easier for all of the towers out there."

Nick Kemper Goes to Nova Scotia (Okay, Not Really)

Parts sellers hear from customers all around the world. At TowPartsNow. com, general manager Nick Kemper recently received a website inquiry from a gentleman in Nova Scotia, a Canadian province located east of Maine — and 3000 miles from Kemper's company in Portland, Ore.

Kemper was home on a weekend and happened to have his laptop open while he was watching some football. A parts request popped up from his Web site: a customer needed a replacement winch. "Since the customer specified the part number, I looked in my parts price file for that winch manufacturer, but I couldn't find it," recalls Kemper.

What was wrong? It turned out that the customer was missing one digit from the part number, so Kemper e-mailed the customer back about it and also provided some ballpark pricing estimates for parts in that category. One phone call later, merchant and customer had agreed on a part and a price.

Now came the tough part of the transaction: Kemper had to get the new winch to the customer's doorstep. "I wasn't sure that the manufacturer would direct-ship the gear to Canada," recalls Kemper. "So I told the customer that I would need to have it shipped to me, and then I would forward it to him." This roundabout method of shipping meant that the customer would have to wait a while for his part. "He was understanding and didn't want to pay for expedited shipping," says Kemper.

Fortunately when Kemper called the manufacturer, he was told that the winch could actually be shipped directly to the customer. "They happily obliged," says a relieved Kemper. "When I got the tracking number, I was able to call the customer and tell him that he was going to get it a lot sooner than expected, which made him very happy."

Kemper enjoys challenges like these. When another customer called to order t-pins for the L-arm of a Chevron wheel lift, he said that he had originally called Kemper's biggest competitor to place his order, but the competitor referred the customer to Kemper's company instead. "That really made me feel good," recalls Kemper, "that we have a reputation for solving problems — even in our biggest competitor's call center!"

Butch Hogland: Growing a Parts Company

Hooks Towing & Recovery Supplies has been in business for over a decade. But believe it or not, Butch Hogland didn't start out with the intention of selling tow truck parts. "Back then I was making sales calls, selling towing equipment," recalls Hogland. "Ninety percent of the customers would always ask about parts — 'Do you have parts?'"

For several months Hogland answered no, but he soon realized that he was being presented with a way to expand his business. "Then it wasn't a question of when," says Hogland, "but 'How do I get started?'" Hogland quickly connected with several parts suppliers and began building an inventory. Then he set up a corporation and launched his new business.

"It has grown so much over the years!" says Hogland. In 2007 he constructed a new building. Two years later he needed to expand, so he added onto the original construction.

Much of the business, says Hogland, involves getting the word out to potential customers. "We work a lot of the trade shows, mail out our catalogs, send out sales flyers," he explains. "We're updating our Web site on a regular basis."

What's in store for the future? Hogland hopes to continue growing his company. "With the great customers we have now," he says, "I think we are well on our way."

Quick Recovery Here and Abroad: Traffic Incident Management in the U.S. and Europe

You roar to a stop in the middle of a maelstrom. Torn metal and spilled fluid scatter across the highway; lights from emergency vehicles flash and spin. Behind you, mile-long columns of cars, trucks and other vehicles sit impatiently, dead in their tracks, their motors idling. Buzzing around the incident site are responders from various agencies — the police department, firefighters, medical providers, a HAZMAT team, to name a few — all desperately trying to clear the accident and get traffic moving again.

The on-scene commander strides over to you. "Get this thing out of here!" he barks, gesturing toward the overturned tanker truck that is blocking two lanes of traffic and most of the gravel shoulder. You nod your head and walk back to your rig. It's going to be a long night.

Managed properly, this incident will be a run-of-the-mill cleanup operation. Tow truck operators are a key component of what's known as Traffic Incident Management, the coordination of resources to identify, respond to and clear adverse events on the roadway. According to David Helman of the Federal Highway Administration, "The top priority is to rescue and remove any injured people, protect responders and the scene, minimize environmental damage, and investigate the incident quickly and thoroughly."

How important is effective traffic incident management? Statistics from the U.S. Department of Transportation show that nonrecurring incidents — traffic accidents, road construction, weather-related slowdowns — cause half of the gridlock and congestion on American highways. Drivers in the most congested urban areas of the United States spend up to 1.3 million hours sitting in traffic every year. The Texas Transportation Institute calculates that on average this costs each driver between $140 and $291 annually. On a national scale, 5.7 billion gallons of gasoline is wasted, and the waiting hours add up to $67.5 billion in lost productivity.

While studying a January 2004 tanker-truck spill in Maryland, Helman noted that "during the nearly 13-hour course of the incident and the following investigation and cleanup, more than 20 responders from over a dozen agencies and private-sector companies were involved onsite." Without solid organization and effective leadership, managing the incident scene can be a coordination nightmare.

The Federal Highway Administration lists five key players involved in traffic incident management: law enforcement, fire and rescue services, emergency medical services (EMS), transportation agencies, towing and recovery services, and hazardous materials contractors. Like any government program, traffic incident management must contend with limited funding, equipment, personnel and shifting political winds from region to region.

When American incident management programs are compared to those of European countries, the differences are often striking. In general, European nations are a step ahead in establishing nationwide systems, whereas in the U.S. various states are still moving toward linking their efforts together in a cross-country program. "Currently, each state is going in a different direction," notes towing expert Bill Jackson. "We don't have cohesive teamwork in the United States."

Despite the obstacles, American agencies are making progress. In Houston, Michael Ogden of Klotz Associates, a consulting engineering firm, is a 20-year veteran of incident management procedures. "I started assisting the Houston Traffic Incident Management Team in 1983," says Ogden. "Since then it's changed from a small group of special event and major incident management responders to the Houston TranStar traffic management center. TranStar houses all of the response agencies and monitors traffic throughout the Houston area."

Launched in 1996, TranStar's goal is to streamline emergency response procedures among the Texas Department of Transportation, local transit authority, and city and county governments. Part of a push to create an Intelligent Transportation System (ITS) across the United States, TranStar also serves as a laboratory of sorts for cutting-edge traffic technology like speed sensors, highway advisory radio, closed-circuit television cameras and dynamic message signs that flash real-time information to drivers.

In Florida, efforts to improve traffic incident management saved local drivers nearly $17 million in one year, according to Bill Jackson. "It's reckoned that for each minute a road can be opened sooner, each driver stuck in the jam can save about five minutes. To put it another way, it could mean the difference between waiting 15 minutes instead of 30 minutes."

Incident management on the international scale can vary depending on the country involved. "Towing in some countries is part of the public agency effort vice the private sector predominant in the United States," notes Ogden, who has worked with incident management programs in Texas, Oklahoma, Montana, and throughout Europe and Asia. "In other words, in those countries it's a government job."

Information crossfeed is particularly important in establishing and improving traffic incident management systems around the world. Countries like the United States, the United Kingdom and the Netherlands periodically send representatives on "scanning tours" and conferences to share tips and techniques.

A major hurdle in the U.S. is the lack of a uniform training and certification program for tow truck operators. "Very few states require [it]," notes a recent report from Atlanta's Traffic Incident Management Enhancement (TIME) task force. "The degree of skill level is left to the owner of the tow company."TIME estimates that it would take $100,000 to create such a program in Georgia. Initiating a nationwide training program for every American city would be no small feat: the Towing & Recovery Association of America estimates that there are between 35,000 and 40,000 tow companies across the 50 states, most with two or three tow trucks and fewer than five employees on the payroll.

For now, local public agencies set minimum requirements including availability, operating hours and basic equipment. Looking into the future, the Federal Highway Administration recommends several actions in its *Traffic Incident Management Handbook*. These include "setting and enforcing maximum response times along with very detailed and specific truck chassis and wrecker specifications that include boom lift capacity, winch and under-lift ratings and rigging and recovery hardware."

Coordination among responders is another critical issue. "Sometimes command personnel from one agency . . . don't always understand the priorities of other agencies," cautions the Federal Highway Administration. "Differing priorities and missions increase the potential conflict and often decrease the effectiveness of response."Towing veteran George Bakker has seen the difficulties firsthand: "You have problems in the big cities, for example, where the police and fire departments butt heads over who's in charge on-site. A lot of times the tow truck operator gets caught in between. That's something that needs to be worked out."

By contrast, several European nations have designated agencies responsible for managing incidents. In Germany, the police force coordinates incident management efforts, and the government has privatized some responders including emergency medical services. To the north in Sweden, firefighters typically take the lead at an incident scene. The American Association of State Highway and Transportation Officials (AASHTO) notes that Sweden has "the unique practice of e-mailing incident scene/victim photos taken with cellular phones to trauma centers prior to EMS' departure from the scene."

Within the United States, 3.5 million square miles of sprawling territory and 160,000 miles of federal highways make it difficult to establish a standardized nationwide system for traffic incident management. Many European nations have a geographic advantage over the U.S., which, for example, is 37 times larger than the United Kingdom. According to Bill Jackson, "In the United Kingdom, which is much smaller, the government has laid down the rules, and it all works very well."

This focus is especially important due to the types of roads in the U.K. The European Road Assessment Programme (EuroRAP), an international nonprofit organization dedicated to improving road safety, reports that while British motorways are well-protected, "single carriageways are generally narrow and have limited visibility" and "British roads appear narrower due to vegetation close to the carriageway and to the greater number of bends and gradients." To assist with incident management, the U.K. Highway Authority launched a "Traffic Officer" program, designating 1,200 personnel to manage events that occur on the roadways.

In the Netherlands, which EuroRAP notes has lower speed limits and traffic volume than Britain, a staggered system of speed indicators allows the federal highway agency to respond immediately to road incidents. Using specially positioned cameras linked to computers, an operator can block lanes and vary speed limits to maneuver traffic more efficiently. Overhead signs mounted every 500 meters (547 yards or about a third of a mile) flash the current speed limit to drivers.

The Dutch Highway Authority created a national response system for all of its highways and important local roads. Protocols were established to improve communication among the various responding agencies. "Probably the most notable aspect of the Dutch program was the uniformity of response among disciplines," noted AASHTO during a recent scanning tour. "Police, fire, EMS, service patrol, and even towing and recovery agents are all trained by a National Traffic and Information Management Center program to ensure uniformity in the handling of calamitous situations."

Tow truck operators participating in the Netherlands program must meet a rigid set of standards. Among other requirements, "operators must wear orange safety clothing, and the tow trucks must have reflective striping," says Rob Dragt, a recovery supervisor in Amsterdam. "All tow trucks here in the Netherlands are painted yellow for safety. No other colors are allowed."

Central to the Netherlands incident management system is a team concept of operations where every event is managed in a generic fashion no matter which responder arrives first. The on-scene commander is appointed on a case-by-case basis depending on the type of incident. To study the best methods of standardizing its approach, the Dutch Highway Authority runs its own test center for traffic systems, where it also trains and certifies personnel who run local traffic operations centers. Says Dragt, "The Dutch incident management system saves a lot of money and time by ensuring quick clearance of blocked highways by a select group of tow truck operators working nationwide."

Neighboring Belgium is currently testing the Netherlands' incident management system. Called the FAST project, the trial run is sponsored by the Ministry of Vlaamse Gemeenschap, the national public works agency. (FAST stands for *Files Aanpakken door Snelle Tussenkomst*, which loosely translated means "quickly tackle traffic jams.") According to Dragt, "The program provides 24-hour patrol and incident management towing on the highways near Antwerp."

The growth of large organizations to coordinate various agencies is a key indicator of the importance of incident management worldwide. In Europe, CENTRICO — the Central European Region Transport Telematics Implementation Coordination Project — brings together five countries to improve intelligent transportation systems and "to enhance international interoperability and harmonization." In the United States, the National Traffic Incident Management Coalition (NTIMC) is working to produce "a joint, national focus" on improving response across the country.

How critical is the need for improving incident management systems in the United States? Data from a previous forum sponsored by the New York Metropolitan Planning Organizations paints a sobering picture: "In the absence of substantial progress, more than 400,000 people will die on the roadways during the current decade at a cost of nearly $2.0 trillion."

An April 2005 report from AASHTO noted that during a scanning tour of several European countries, "each country reported a significant projected increase in highway usage over the next several years." Because of this, "each country's transportation industry recognized that it could no longer 'build its way out of congestion' and that proper management of roadway and personnel resources was necessary to offset the tremendous economic and quality of life issues resulting from congestion."

With Europe taking the lead in establishing networked, national incident management programs, the United States has some catching up to do. The benefits of building an effective traffic incident management program are enormous. In fact, the Texas Transportation Institute notes that successful coordination among agencies can shave at least 40 percent off the time it takes to clear a major incident. With traffic flow increasing on roads all around the globe, effective management of road incidents can make all the difference. For tow truck operators, getting to the incident site and getting to work is critical. "In situations where you need a specific type of vehicle to clear an incident," says George Bakker, "the tow operator has the equipment that can save somebody's life."

Two Styles of Tow Truck:
European and American Models

Big or small? When comparing American and European tow trucks, the first thing you'll notice is a difference in size. Visiting Europeans are often struck by how much larger many things are in the United States, from meals to cars to buildings — and the tow truck is no exception. Rob Dragt, a recovery supervisor based in Amsterdam, puts it succinctly: "American tow trucks are big — very big — because in the U.S. there are wide highways with a lot of room to maneuver. But here in the Netherlands and other parts of Europe, roads are narrow and you have no room for a big wrecker on the road."

There are also differences in the manufacturing process. In the Netherlands, for example, tow trucks are built to order on a new or secondhand chassis, notes Dragt. "The Dutch do not build on an assembly line like the U.S. because the market for tow trucks isn't as big here." In addition, because they operate on narrow roads, European tow trucks are built with a shorter wheelbase than their American counterparts, with ballast in the front to steady the vehicle.

In the early days, European towing firms often used American vehicles for their day-to-day operations. "American trucks were heavier, more fortified and had steel front bumpers," notes George Bakker, who operates 60 trucks in Arizona, Utah and New York. "At first, European tow trucks used a thinner front bumper and their suspensions weren't as robust as American trucks." Dragt notes that operators in the U.K. often used twin booms like the Holmes 750, while the Dutch preferred smaller cranes built by Garwood or Austin Western.

Over time, European manufacturers reworked their vehicles and initiated a number of improvements that eventually made their way to American shores. In the years following World War II, Ernest Holmes, Jr., father of the American tow truck, proposed a cradle-type mechanism for wreckers. However, because of American operators' reliance on the tow bar, Holmes' idea failed to catch on. Europe moved ahead and began mass-producing that type of mechanism, says Bakker. So while trucks in the U.S. still used a traditional hook-and-chain mechanism, European models began sporting the wheel lift, which used a yoke that cradled the recovered vehicle's axle or tires. Boosting the wheel lift's effectiveness was another fairly new technology: hydraulics. "A good example of this was the Swedish EKA wrecker," notes Bakker.

Basing its design on the forklift truck, EKA fitted a hydraulically powered boom that, using various attachments, raised the recovered vehicle off the ground. The first model of the EKA wheel lift was unveiled in 1960. In the United States, the wheel lift system was first offered as an add-on for overhead cranes, and later as part of the wrecker itself.

Bill Bottoms led the charge for hydraulic tow trucks in America by creating and mass-producing the Challenger Wrecker. "There was such a tremendous surge in sales that other companies like Holmes and Century followed suit," recalls Bakker. "Then half a dozen smaller manufacturers jumped on the bandwagon." Meanwhile, the hook-and-chain system eventually went out of style in the U.S. to be replaced with the wheel lift mechanism, although the hook-and-chain is still used in situations where the wheel lift is not feasible.

Bakker remembers the change with some irony. "It took about 20 to 25 years for the U.S. to catch on to the wheel lift," he says. "In fact, I was one of the proponents of keeping the tow bar. I thought the wheel lift was a passing fancy. Much to my amazement, now it's gone completely in the opposite direction and the wheel lift is the weapon of choice, so to speak."

As American vehicles took on more aerodynamic styling, tow trucks adapted as well. U.S. manufacturers fashioned thinner metal bumpers or used a different material altogether— fiberglass or another engineering-grade plastic. Today, many American vehicles must be recovered with a wheel lift to avoid damaging their plastic bumpers. "With non-metal bodywork you can't use a chain to lift, or you'll destroy the bodywork," notes Dragt.

During the past decade a new addition to the American towing industry has been the rotator tow truck, a cousin to the hydraulic truck crane. These giant vehicles blend tow-truck capability with a large crane for recovery operations. While useful for heavy-duty work, rotators are sometimes too big for their own good. "The weight of the truck crane is a limitation," says Bakker. "At a large radius, the crane is limited in what it can pick up. Too much and the rotator might tip over."

In addition, boom length on a rotator truck might be too short for the job: "Most of the booms are in the 30- to 40-foot range, and some manufacturers offer an additional extension or jib." The weight ceiling established under federal law means that many rotators are at or over their allowable weight. "It would be nice to have a national weight exemption like fire engines have," notes Bakker. In addition, he cautions that the cost of purchasing a rotator can be prohibitive: "Large rotating tow trucks start at about $250,000 and can run to half a million dollars each. As an operator you could have a monthly mortgage payment of over $10,000."

Today, most modern European tow trucks are equipped with a wheel lift and a knuckle-boom hydraulic crane — a European innovation — folded behind the cab. Originally crafted by Hiab in Helsinki, Finland, the gear was adapted with a boom-and-sling arrangement to pick up a vehicle and transfer it to the recovery vehicle.

Although he owns mostly American-made tow trucks, George

Bakker puts a lot of faith into European models as well. "I use a unit called the Bulldog Interstater, which was imported from Europe by Bill Jackson," says Bakker. "I also have two unbelievable American units from Norbert Bertling, who builds the Trebron wheel lift truck. I've used them for 10 years and never put a nickel into them. They're bulletproof."

Exporting Used Tow Trucks
to Central and South America

Over the years, the United States has done a lot of business with Central and South America, trading everything from fruit to oil to machinery. Vehicle exports are also part of the profitable import/export market. In 2005, the U.S. Department of Commerce reported that American manufacturers exported over $4.2 billion worth of vehicles to Latin America and the Caribbean. Some of these vehicles have been tow trucks, both used and new. How have American manufacturers and towers penetrated the Central and South American market, and why do some of them believe that increasing overseas sales benefits American towers' reputations as well as their pocketbooks?

FleetTruckParts.com, headquartered in Calumet Park, Ill., began fabricating heavy-duty tow trucks under the name WayneBuilt in 1970 and sells medium and heavy-duty equipment and parts, including factory surplus, used trucks, salvage vehicles and major truck component cores. During the 1980s the company expanded its sales markets to Mexico, Central America, South America, Africa and the Middle East. "We originally got into the truck export market to serve a growing need for American-made trucks, equipment and parts in the world marketplace," says Rob Bramlette, president of FleetTruckParts.com. The successful business was built through old-fashioned word-of-mouth, as export buyers learned about the company from fellow importers.

Over the last three decades, FleetTruckParts.com has engaged in direct exports and has also sourced specific inventory from around the U.S. for its customers. The company's overseas buyers come from one of two camps, says Bramlette. "We sell to importers who are end users of the equipment. We also sell to importers who serve as 'middle men' and supply their marketplaces with American trucks, equipment and parts."

Although towers around the world share similar responsibilities on the road, there are subtle differences in the equipment they use. "Most towing companies in Central and South America are no different from what we find in the United States," notes Tom Griffin, director of export and government sales for Miller Industries in Ooltewah, Tenn. "There are small, medium and large companies, some more professional than others, all competing for business." However, says Griffin, much of the vehicle fleet in those regions is older than that of the average American towing firm — many Central and South American towers still operate classic Holmes 600 and 750 series wreckers, for example.

Over the years, however, Griffin has noticed a gradual change in the tow truck export business. "The middle class is growing," he notes, and is purchasing new vehicles like those offered in the United States. "When you travel the streets of Mexico City, Quito, Caracas or Sao Paulo, people are driving Camrys, Tahoes, Muranos, Explorers and so on," observes Griffin.

As for trucks, new class-8 models include Volvo, Renault, Mercedes, MAN and Scania, "as well as Freightliner, International and Kenworth models found here in North America." When one of these vehicles breaks down or is involved in an accident, tow operators need the latest technology to perform effective recovery operations. Because of the expense involved in purchasing new equipment, towers in Central and

226

South America are making the jump to new technology in a gradual fashion. "Economics do not allow them to change their entire fleets at once," says Griffin. "However, when it's time to replace a vehicle, they fully understand what is available on the market. They look to buy the best equipment possible."

In addition to the high cost, exporting tow trucks requires coordination with various governments, each with its own set of rules. In addition to obtaining an export license from the U.S. Department of Commerce, American exporters are subject to import duties, value-added tax (VAT), plus other taxes and fees levied by the countries receiving the exported goods. Colombia, for example, levies a 15 percent import duty on foreign goods. The costs can add up quickly.

Certain countries place additional restrictions on their import sales. Gary Coe, partner in Golden West Towing Equipment of Anaheim, Calif., recalls a bulk sale of tow trucks to Mexico in 2004: "We sold somewhere between 14 and 17 trucks," he says. "The government stipulated that the trucks had to have model years between 1995 and 1998." Once the trucks were verified as the appropriate vintage, the rest of the transaction went smoothly. "Our buyer wired the money, and we shipped the trucks via transporter using a driver who was authorized for international transport."

At Miller Industries, Tom Griffin has noticed an increase in regulations enforced by Central and South American governments. Some of the newer rules are driven by ecological concerns. "Most of the major cities in Latin and South America suffer from the same smog and pollution as our cities here in the United States," says Griffin. "In fact, most of them have a much older vehicle population, and pollution levels are considerably worse." To reduce toxic emissions, governments have placed restrictions on the importation of older vehicles. In addition, many countries have their own truck assembly factories, so limiting imports helps support their domestic economies.

From a purely business perspective, navigating the roadblocks toward establishing and growing an export business is worth the effort, says Gary Coe. "If American distributors could increase the number of used tow trucks exported to Central and South America," he says, "it would change the economics of our industry considerably." According to Coe, the reputation of the American tow industry is hampered by good tow truck drivers who are not businesspeople. They launch towing businesses by purchasing inexpensive used tow trucks. "Because these trucks are cheap, untrained opportunists, towing predators and weak businessmen just jump easily into the business. They make the good guys look bad because of their ethics or pricing," laments Coe.

Tow firms that are shutting down or upgrading their vehicle fleet jettison thousands of wreckers every year in the U.S. — many of which are snapped up by new towing firms with less-than-respectable pedigrees. "It's a snowball effect," says Alan Francisco, owner of Francisco Towing in Bensalem, Penn. "These fly-by-night tow firms buy cheap used tow trucks, charge really low rates, then crash their trucks or damage the vehicles they're recovering," he says. "The insurance company handles a $2 million payout for damages, and then everyone's insurance rates go up."

Because of this problem, an increased emphasis on exporting used tow trucks would greatly benefit the American towing industry, says Coe. He theorizes that since an increase in used truck exports would drop the available supply in the United States, the resulting shortage would make it difficult for opportunists to start towing businesses on the cheap. This "weeding out" of low-reputation towing companies would be of great advantage to those towers who do the job right. "Low-end towers would then be forced to qualify for financing on *new* trucks," says Coe — a much more expensive proposition. "When you have cheap tow trucks, it makes it too easy to get into the industry."

In addition to quick-buck artists, Coe points to what he calls "uneducated, non-business savvy towers" who, after years of doing great work for a towing firm, open their own business but charge low rates as if they're still working for wages somewhere else. "Some of these towers — who don't know any better — are working right out of their apartments," he says, often for auto clubs and cut-rate prices. "Yes they have a truck, yes they have insurance, but the auto clubs will never step up to competitive prices as long as there's a backlog of people looking for towing contracts at cheap rates." Coe has seen many small towing firms come and go: because of their low rates, some new companies struggle financially, their equipment gets repossessed, and then another tower picks up the vacated assignment. Higher prices on equipment would keep these towers from suffering, says Coe. "If, for example, everyone had to buy a new truck or one that was no more than three years old, it would change the situation considerably."

Importers from Central and South America have taken the initiative in purchasing used wreckers in the United States. In his Pennsylvania town, Alan Francisco has noticed that businesspeople from other countries are purchasing used trucks and parts, then shipping the merchandise back home to sell. "They buy the older stuff, and then overseas it goes," says Francisco. While he respects the business savvy of such purchases, Francisco argues that American manufacturers and distributors should do more to take advantage of the market for overseas sales of used tow trucks. "The major manufacturers are primarily focused on selling new tow trucks," he says. "If they'd look at selling used trucks, there would be a lot fewer junk trucks around."

Rob Bramlette points to another benefit of an increased export market: "The American tow truck manufacturers make the best equipment in the business," he says with pride. "So when you're selling it in a global marketplace, it helps to have that brand-name recognition and quality manufacturing behind the equipment. As export volume rises, it provides crucial jobs for the American worker." Thanks to the established export network for American trucks and equipment, adds Bramlette, "a piece of equipment that might otherwise bring in little or no money, or sell at a scrap price, will often retain a higher resale value." Preparing tow trucks for export creates jobs in the U.S. including truckers, dismantlers and salespeople, creating a "win-win situation," he adds.

In addition, Central and South American towers' needs for up-to-date towing technology help boost export sales of both used and new tow trucks. "The population of new vehicles drives the demand for our modern towing and recovery equipment," remarks Tom Griffin. But since not every tower can afford brand-new equipment, the market for used equipment will continue its steady sales as well. "There is a market for good used equipment with the more recent technology," says Griffin. "Even in smaller markets the end users are familiar with the technology, and will still be looking for good deals on used equipment."

What does the future of used tow truck exporting look like? Tom

Griffin sees strong demand for used and new towing equipment, "but the buyers will be smarter, looking to buy quality, technology and something with readily available spare parts." For Rob Bramlette, business — in both old and new tow trucks — has been on the upswing. "But," he cautions, "as foreign competition increases, it will be up to U.S. towing manufacturers to continue producing a competitive product at competitive prices. Good service and selection will keep the export business alive through the up and down cycles of the export business."

Here and There:
World Recovery Techniques

Tom Luciano looks out across his audience and breaks into a smile. "This is our chance to dig in and get dirty!" he says, pointing at the crowd of towers in front of him. Everyone is dressed for combat; their trucks stand ready nearby. The goal? To share information about recovery techniques by performing a live demonstration on a disabled vehicle brought in for the occasion. The information that participating towers glean from the exercise will be shared across the nation — and, quite possibly, around the world.

A respected training instructor and inductee in the International Towing and Recovery Hall of Fame in Chattanooga, Tenn., Tom Luciano is celebrating his 36th year in the towing industry. He works for Miller Industries, headquartered in Ooltewah, Tenn., but is rarely in the home office. Whether training 150 drivers in Texas on the finer points of recovery operations or demonstrating how to rescue a loaded cement mixer from underneath a garbage truck in Las Vegas, Luciano is constantly on the move, sharing his expertise with tow operators around the nation. Cross-flow of information among towers is critical to improving the tower's craft, says Luciano. "You always want to stay current. You don't want to get behind."

As part of his mission to share the wealth, Luciano launched a seminar titled "Brainstorming with the Pros." Packed with discussions and demonstrations, the workshop has received rave reviews. "As I have traveled all over the world," says Luciano, "towers are always asking me, 'How would other towers have handled this casualty?' The pros in Florida want to know how the towers in Michigan would handle this. The towers in Canada ask how the guys in the 'States would have handled their wreck. I have been asked these questions so many times that I decided to put together a program to address them."

Luciano's most recent large-scale presentations of "Brainstorming with the Pros" occurred recently in Florida and at the American Towman Exposition in Baltimore. He also presents workshops to smaller groups of towers on a regular basis.

Although Luciano's loaded schedule already has him dashing from one end of the country to the other, he works constantly to keep his "Brainstorming" sessions fresh and inventive. Since many towers shoot digital photos of their work for purposes of education, documentation, and insurance, Luciano built his seminar around a visual presentation of recovery operations from around the world. "For the most part," he says, "towers learn more from a series of photos than from reading written text." Luciano believes that photographic evidence is a highly effective learning tool — perhaps *the* most effective.

To drive his point home, Luciano requires all attendees at "Brainstorming with the Pros" to bring photographs of at least one recent recovery operation. "The photos need to be from start to finish of any type of recovery job," says Luciano, "big or small." This not only personalizes the seminar but also allows Luciano to ensure the most up-to-date program possible.

In preparation for the class, Luciano instructs the participants to arrive in work gear and to bring their trucks with them. Being ready with the proper clothing, equipment, and vehicle is critical for the second half of the workshop, which involves hands-on demonstrations of the techniques discussed. At this point in the program, Luciano breaks the attendees into smaller groups.

The recovery demonstrations can vary widely. Several years ago a class with the Oklahoma Wrecker Owners Association (OWOA) took place at the Oklahoma City Police and Fire Training Center. "Tommy Luciano is an excellent instructor," says Chris Puckett, president of the association. "No matter what size of truck or recovery, there is always something special to learn."

In an interesting twist, during the workshop OWOA presented Luciano with a challenging scenario: pulling construction equipment out of a river. "Dewey Farrington, one of our vice presidents, located a bulldozer and some other construction equipment," says Puckett. "We found a river bottom so we could drop the equipment in, to see how Tommy would get it out. Dewey ran a loaded dump truck in the river. It was very sandy so the wheels were buried pretty good. Then Dewey and Tommy worked on the setups for the class."

Over the years American towers and their overseas counterparts have traded ideas, equipment, and stories of tricky recovery jobs. But there are marked differences in how domestic and international towing firms handle traffic incidents. "Most industrialized countries use wreckers that are similar in size and design," says Jack Schrock, who like Luciano is a Towing Hall of Fame inductee. "Many of the designs we use in America were adapted from European models," he adds. "As a result, our recovery techniques can follow closely with theirs." Given this, many of the differences result from environmental constraints — colder weather, narrower roads, different traffic patterns.

During the past five years, recovery operations in the United Kingdom have been centralized under the national Highways Agency. According to Liz Talbot, project lead for the traffic incident management program, the U.K.'s transportation network "includes various types of road ranging from motorways carrying up to 200,000 vehicles per day to single carriageway trunk roads (the major A roads) carrying fewer than 10,000 vehicles per day." The National Traffic Control Centre (NTCC) monitors traffic round-the-clock via 1,730 closed-circuit television cameras positioned across the network. Recovery specialists on contract are required to respond within 30 minutes for small vehicles and 45 minutes for larger ones.

A key characteristic of roads overseas is their tight width. Compared with American towers, who sometimes operate on six-lane highways and generous suburban streets, European operators often find themselves with little room in which to maneuver. This characteristic affects the equipment they use. "Due to narrow roadways in Europe, their tow trucks are shorter than ours," says Luciano, "and very often have tandem steering axles. This helps them turn in tighter corners and narrow intersections." Because of this, towers in countries like England are able to handle their recovery scenarios differently from their American counterparts. Due to the length of the average American wrecker, the driver might have difficulty getting his or her truck square with the disabled vehicle. Wreckers in the U.K., on the other hand, have an easier time squeezing into tight spaces and utilize side-pulling to rescue disabled vehicles.

Sometimes overseas towing firms avoid using wreckers entirely. In Japan, for example, towers often use cranes instead of tow trucks for heavy-duty recovery. "The process is quite different there as a result," says Schrock. Moreover, he explains, halfway around the world, the towing industry isn't necessarily as advanced as we've come to expect. "In some developing countries of the former Russian bloc," notes Schrock, "towers did not even have wreckers. Esa Pyyhkalainen, a friend of mine from Finland, opened a towing and recovery business in Estonia, where he says they had previously used only horses, chains, and blocks for a recovery job."

Due to geography and road design, the Netherlands has towers who are frequently able to make use of mobile cranes to lift disabled vehicles, much like their Japanese counterparts. Since the Netherlands are a much smaller country than the United States —just 1/230th the size — it's much easier to get from point to point. Therefore mobile cranes can be dispatched and arrive at an incident scene with great speed.

Dutch tow supervisor Rob Dragt describes one recovery job where a mobile crane saved the day: "A truck was pulling a drawbar trailer loaded with two 20-foot box-shaped containers packed with scrap metal."

The driver turned too quickly around the curve of the major two-lane highway on which he was traveling, overturning the truck. Worse yet, the vehicle crashed onto the emergency lane. The national highway agency shut down the highway until the truck could be lifted off the asphalt.

Due to the narrowness of the road, recovery specialists were unable to pull the truck upright with a straight winch. Instead, to assist the tow truck already on scene, they called in a mobile crane with a 60-ton capacity. "First the crane lifted and lowered the self-lift system from the container on the truck," explains Dragt. "Later the crane was used as a restrainer to 'catch' the truck after it was winched over." The crane also assisted with tipping the overturned container into an upright position.

"In the Netherlands it's easy to call in a mobile crane with a lot of lifting capacity," says Dragt. "It's difficult to recover a big 18-wheeler using a recovery truck, but it's an easy job with one or two mobile cranes. Distances are not the same as in the United States."

Looking beyond recovery techniques, Jack Schrock notes another huge difference between American and European towers that, left unchecked, he believes will do irreparable damage to the American towing industry. Schrock has noticed that for overseas towers, "there is much more 'business' in the business."

According to Schrock, American towers focus more on operational technique than on the business and marketing techniques of their trade. "For example," he says, "while attending a meeting of the International Federation of Recovery Specialists in Belgium, without exception everyone there was in a suit and tie with professional business skills that go far beyond just operating a wrecker."

Schrock also brings up another concern: that unless American towers think about business first, the towing industry could fall under the auspices of local government rather than continue as private contractors. "I'm concerned that we could see wreckers in firehouses in the future," says Schrock. "Los Angeles has already started that trend." Schrock also points to the insertion of the ambulance into the firehouse during the 1970s, noting that Los Angeles was the first to implement the approach before it spread across the country. He is concerned that the same trend could take hold with tow trucks.

As we've already seen, governments in countries like the United

Kingdom are taking greater control of how tow trucks are integrated into their traffic management methods. Can the same thing happen in the U.S.? "Government at different levels is already going into the towing and recovery business," says Schrock, who points to government owned-and-operated wreckers in New York City and Chicago.

The Illinois department of transportation implemented the Minutemen Emergency Traffic Patrol program in 1960 to cut down on clearance time for traffic accidents and obstructions on interstate highways. Prior to that time, motorists or responding law enforcement personnel often had to call for a wrecker themselves. With the Minutemen program, government-owned emergency vehicles — including specially designed heavy tow trucks — respond as a unit to traffic incidents.

"Business management is an uncomfortable process for many American towers, but recovery techniques are not," says Schrock. "Therefore we usually want to talk only about what we know, rather than what we need to know. Due to American towers' emphasis on operational technique rather than business development, says Schrock, "the annual failure rate in towing and recovery businesses can be as high as 25 percent."

Back at his latest seminar for towers, Tom Luciano stresses the importance of worldwide communication and training among towers. For the three decades that he has worked in the towing and recovery business, Luciano's watchword has always been "prepare." But he cautions that the training only provides so much: "You can't pre-plan for a wreck, any more than you can plan for a fire," he says.

"We can never pre-plan, duplicate in class, or critique ourselves on how to handle a casualty if we haven't seen something like it previously." Luciano encourages towers to take what they've learned from his workshop and adapt the techniques to real-life recovery operations as needed: "You can't spread the education unless people are willing to share what they do."

§

About the Author

Allan T. Duffin is a freelance writer and television/multimedia producer. He writes books and Internet, magazine, and newspaper articles. For television he has written, produced, co-produced, and developed programs for the History and Discovery networks. Allan is a veteran of the U.S. Air Force. Visit his website at www.aduffin.com.

Books by Allan T. Duffin, available at Amazon.com

Catch the Sky: The Adventures and Misadventures of a Police Helicopter Pilot
Duffin Creative

History in Blue: 160 Years of Women Police, Sheriffs, Detectives, and State Troopers
Kaplan Publishing/Simon & Schuster

The "12 O'Clock High" Logbook: The Unofficial History of the Novel, Motion Picture, and Television Series
BearManor Media

Tow Truck Kings: Secrets of the Towing & Recovery Business
Available from Amazon.com

Tow Truck Kings 2: More Secrets of the Towing & Recovery Business
Available from Amazon.com

TheatreBook: A Compact Guide to Running Your Theatre
Available from Amazon.com

Made in the USA
Monee, IL
18 August 2024

64117874R00138